A
HISTORY
OF
TEMPLE, GEORGIA

A West Georgia Town
of Carroll County

D1560604

Settled in 1882   Chartered in 1883

Burell Williams Holder
and
Ruth Roberts Holder

Vabella Publishing
P.O. Box 1052
Carrollton, Georgia 30112
www.vabella.com

Front Cover: Welcome to Temple Sign, 2011, Courtesy of Author
Back Cover: Sage Street Stores, Circa 1890, Courtesy, Burt Stevens

Manufactured in the United States of America

13-digit ISBN 978-1-938230-41-7

Library of Congress Control Number 2013907923

10 9 8 7 6 5 4 3 2 1

CONTENTS

Robert Henry Temple, 1831-1901
"He was a man of fine physique, modest and unassuming,
firm of character, and of the highest integrity: a type of the
noblest of the Virginia gentlemen."
The Richmond Dispatch, December 24, 1901

CHAPTER I

AN INTRODUCTION

Temple is a small, west Georgia city transversed by the Southern Railroad and the Bankhead Highway (U.S. 78) with both thoroughfares running in an east-west direction. Georgia Highway 113 runs through the heart of town from Carrollton to Draketown.

The city is forty-five miles west of Atlanta, the capital of the state. It is located in the northeastern part of Carroll County and is twelve miles north of Carrollton, the county seat. Interstate Highway 20 runs through the southern part of the city. The elevation is approximately 1200 feet and the climate is mild with an abundant rainfall.

Temple was settled alongside newly laid railroad tracks 130 years ago as a small, agricultural village. The year was 1882 and the chief crop was cotton. To a lesser extent, corn, wheat and oats were grown.

The economic success of this place was gauged by the amount of cotton produced and the price it brought. A good crop and a good price meant a healthy buying power for farmers and, in turn, this brought financial success to the merchants. Farmers paid their debts on time in good years and bought a bit more extravagantly with their extra "cotton money." The economy was characterized by a dual dependence between the cotton farmer and the local merchant. A large part of the success of this credit and barter system was in the form of mutual faith and trust.

This book is a revision and update of *A History of Temple, Georgia,* published in 1982. New materials and photos were added. Excerpts from a copy of a recently discovered issue of *The Temple Enterprise,* Temple's only newspaper, were also included.

An attempt has been made to portray the area as it was during the last 130 years. Research has been a joint endeavor that involved local citizens, former members, and even strangers. The people shared their memories of the yesterdays of Temple by recalling happenings of days gone by. They were able to capture, once again, the very atmosphere of this area when everyone's livelihood depended upon old King Cotton. The citizens found old photographs, school records, newspapers, and other treasures in places where they had been tucked away many years ago.

Many other sources of information were used in gleaning the historical facts about the first years of Temple. Bit by bit, from near and faraway places, exciting facts were learned and placed in sequence in order to paint a true picture of this small city and its surroundings.

A special interest was to learn about Robert Henry Temple, for whom the town was named. A big breakthrough came when contact was made with Weldon Cannon, a history professor at Temple Junior College, Temple, Texas. Through his wealth of knowledge of the Temple family and from sources in Virginia, a vivid account of Robert Henry Temple was realized. Locating a photograph of the man for whom our town is named was also a dream come true.

However, all of the worthwhile and interesting facts concerning the town have not been unveiled, and perhaps they never will. But this does not bring despair, for it is good to leave something untold, to stir our imaginations, or to leave something just to wonder about.

The story of Temple is a simple one, and is herein simply told. Nevertheless, this does not lessen the importance of this soil, for Temple and the surrounding communities represent an important foundation upon which this great state and nation were built.

In the fall of 1883, E. Lewis Connell, a young schoolmaster at Temple Academy, depicted the tempo and spirit of the town when he wrote the following poem. It appeared in the January 4, 1884, edition of the *Carroll Free Press*. It is presented here in memory of Lewis Connell and all the early settlers who built this place many years ago.

Temple

Mid Carroll's rich and fertile lands
    About one year ago
Where our little town now stands
    Was but a house or two.

How quick and fast they built our town
    Why it was just last fall
That on this very plot of ground
    Just one store house was all.

But ah! that number soon enlarged,
    And many settlers came
Copeland and Sewell, McCain and Barge
    Have here sought wealth and fame.

There's Williams and Mobley, Brooks and Bell
    Who's also took a part,
Griffin and Enterkin will always tell
    Our merchants keep in heart.

And now we hear the bellows blow,
    The blacksmith's hammer sound;
A drug store owned by Brooks and Rowe
    Is now within our town.

We know our town it not so large,
    Our citizens though are pure,
For Favor, and Holland, Davis, and Barge
    Success is almost sure.

We've worked our streets that were so rough,
    And leveled down the bumps,
Although to us 'twas very tough
    To dig up all the stumps.

The grandest city of our land,
    Like Temple was once quite small,
And on the spot where she now stands,
    There was no house at all.

Let us while prospects sweetly smile,
    Begin to persevere,
And each with energy arise,
    And build a city here.

CHAPTER II

THE CREEKS

The native inhabitants of this section of northwestern Georgia at the time of the arrival of European settlers were the Creek Indians. The vast forest land which they owned was called the Creek Nation. The name "Creek" was given by the English because of the many small streams beside which the Indians lived. Paths traveled by the Native inhabitants were known to exist on both sides and running parallel to the Little Tallapoosa River from Paulding County through the Temple vicinity and onward into Alabama.

For many years, prior the establishment of Carroll County, European settlers lived among the Natives. Through the years, the Creeks began to live more and more like the Europeans, and some of the Native women became their wives. The Chief of the Cowetas, a leading subtribal group, was William McIntosh, the son of a Creek Indian mother and Scotch father.

By the 1820s, the Creeks had adopted, somewhat, the manner and dress of the European settlers. Many were speaking broken English, and a few of their children had been taught to read and write the language. They cultivated vegetables and fruits; they raised cattle, hogs, and poultry. Small patches of cotton were also grown. The Creeks hunted the abundant wild game, fished the sparkling clear streams, and gathered fruits and nuts produced by the forest.

In the early 1800s, the new settlers began more and more to want possession of the land of the Creeks. Consequently, after a period of persistent persuasion, treaties with the Indians ceded land to the U.S. Government. European settlers moved in from older parts of Georgia, cleared small plots of land, and established farms.

In 1825, at Indian Springs, Georgia, Chief McIntosh signed a treaty which ceded the land that included what is now Carroll County. Wealthy McIntosh reserved his home acreage, Acorn Bluff, near Whitesburg since he did not plan to move.

All of the Creek Indians did not approve of the treaty which provided an exchange of their land for equal acreage in the West. They were also to be paid for the improvements on the ceded land.

Angered at McIntosh for signing the treaty, a band of Upper Creeks known as "Red Sticks" was dispatched from Alabama for the purpose of killing him. They successfully carried out their mission in the early hours of May 1, 1825. They surrounded his house, killed him, and then burned the large plantation home. The hostile Indians plundered through the possessions of McIntosh for several days. After they left, friends buried his body across the road.

The brokenhearted Lower Creeks reluctantly made their way westward to their new homes west of the Mississippi. Many of them never reached their new hunting ground; they died during the long, hard journey.

Though it has been more than one hundred seventy-five years since the Creeks departed, reminders of their time here are still present. During farming days numerous arrowheads and bits of pottery were unearthed by the plows. Even today an old arrowhead is found occasionally, giving proof once again, that the Creeks hunted the wild game here many years ago.

CHAPTER III

EARLY CARROLL COUNTY

On December 11, 1826, the act which created Carroll County was passed. The new county was named for Charles Carroll of Maryland, a signer of the Declaration of Independence.

When Carroll County was first laid out in 1827, it included a vast area much larger than Carroll County is today. In later years parts of the original county were cut away and became parts of Heard, Douglas, Troup, Campbell, and Haralson Counties.

Within the original boundaries of Carroll County there were 1,600 square miles. This land was distributed by the lottery system at Milledgeville in 1827. At the time, Milledgeville was the capital of Georgia. Among others, bachelors who had reached their 18th birthday, were United States citizens, and had lived in the state at least three years were entitled to one lottery ticket. Others meeting certain qualifications were given two tickets. Veterans of the Revolution, widows and orphans of veterans killed in one of the wars, and certain other groups received special consideration.

The land lots were composed of 202 ½ acres. Those who drew lots paid a fee of $18 per lot. All fractional lots were withheld from the lottery and sold later at public auction.

The land lots were considered very poor and almost worthless in the early days. Only a few of the richest spots were selected for farming. The other land was very cheap with some selling for less than ten cents per acre. Holders of successful lottery tickets generally sold their lots very cheaply. A bed quilt, gun, dog, or cow was swapped for an entire lot of 202 ½ acres. An innkeeper refused an offer of a land lot in exchange for a night's lodging. It was nothing unusual for men to stake whole lots in small wagers, or to give two hundred acres to "boot" in a horse trade.

Many of the drawees of Carroll County lots never moved to the county. Most of those who did were from the cotton-growing section of Middle Georgia.

The law provided that the freeholders living in the new county could meet on the first Monday in May of 1827 to elect county officials. This meeting was held at the McIntosh Reserve near Whitesburg. Five justices of the Inferior Court, a county clerk, sheriff, tax collector, tax receiver, coroner, and a surveyor were selected.

The first Carroll County Inferior Court met May 31, 1827. In June, the justices of the court who had charge of the roads, bridges, and all public property met again and authorized one of their number to buy a lot in the Fifth District for a county seat. A lot was bought from land lot 115 from Thomas Bolton near where Sand Hill is today. This place later came to be known as "Old Carrollton."

After much of the county had been cut away by the legislature and added to other counties, the county seat was no longer situated near the center of the county. For that reason, on November 14, 1829, the county seat was moved to its present site in the Tenth District, land lot number 128. The new site was first named Troupsville, in honor of Governor George M. Troup. On December 22 the state legislature incorporated the new county seat under the name of Carrollton rather than Troupsville.

Carroll County was settled in the true spirit of the pioneer. Many of the settlers were young men who had the stamina, courage, and desire to challenge the wilderness and reap a living from its soil.

The early pioneers of Carroll County were confronted by a problem much more severe than the forest which did not give way easily to be felled, cleared, and cultivated. This was a lawless group of thieves and desperadoes known as the Pony Club, since their chief crime was stealing horses and sometimes cattle. During the day, the thieves appeared to be honest neighbors; at night they stole. The Pony Club hid stolen horses in swamps and thickets until they could be slipped out and driven to market. At times they were known to hide horses in a canebrake in Almon's pasture at Buckhorn Tavern.

If resisted, the thieves were always armed and ready to protect their stolen animals. They terrorized the entire county, and no man knew when his life might be threatened by these renegades. The early pioneers had to be constantly aware of their horses' whereabouts, for to have them stolen at night left no beast to pull the plow.

The early settlers, out of necessity, eventually abandoned the slow justice of the early courts and established their own law presided over by Judge Lynch.

Vigilance committees, known as The Slicks, were organized to combat the menace of the Pony Club. The Slicks fought the outlaws constantly. The leaders of the Slicks were called Captain Slick. One of these famous captains was Sloman Wynn of Hickory Level.

At every election, muster day, or any public gathering the Pony Club was on hand drinking, cursing, and raising fights while their fellow members were on the outskirts stealing horses.

When a horse was stolen the Slicks did not wait for the sheriff or constable, but got on the trail themselves, recovered the horse and brought the thief to trial.

The Slicks soon found that warrants, arrests, and trials as the law directed were of no avail since the club was always ready at the trial of one of their members with witnesses to prove an alibi. The Slicks had no choice but to become a law unto themselves. When a Pony Club member was caught he was whipped with a hickory and advised to leave the county or the next time they would "hurt" him.

No disguises were worn by the Slicks. Every settler was known as a member of one side or the other. Their farms were side by side, they traded at the same stores, sat on the same juries, and cast their ballots in the same boxes.

At the last fight, no member of the Slicks was seriously hurt and only one member of the Pony Club was killed. He was shot while attempting to escape with a stolen horse, near where Hickory Level is today. The horse thieves were driven from the county. Some, though, mended their ways and remained as law-abiding citizens.

The farmer could now rest at night for he no longer feared for his life or that when morning dawned his horses would be gone.

In the 1830s, Majors and Coltharp sold goods near the banks of the Little Tallapoosa River about one and one-half miles from Hart Town. The goods were brought in from Augusta by wagons. Iron and steel were brought here by the settlers to be hammered into farming implements. Plows, hames, swingtree irons, axes, and horseshoes were forged out by the county blacksmiths.

For forty-odd years after the settlement of the northeastern Carroll County, log-rollings provided a means of getting rid of logs on the farms. Quiltings planned to coincide with the log-rollings afforded a day of visiting for the women.

Only the undergrowth and small trees were cut when a farm was first cleared. The large trees were killed by cutting through the bark near the ground and was called "deadening." A few years later the dead trees would be blown down by the wind or fall due to the base rotting away. Before planting time, the farmers would invite the neighbors to help roll the logs into a great heap where they were burned.

The women of the settlement were invited to a quilting at the farmer's home on the day of the log-rolling. The women cooked a sumptuous dinner because the men and boys had hearty appetites after working all morning in the "new ground."

Beautiful and serviceable quilts were made by the women when they gathered around the quilting frame which had been lowered from the loft. The quilts were piled high on the beds at night when the fires died down to coals and the bedrooms became icy cold.

Hog killing time was held during the cold spells of fall and winter. The neighbors "swapped" work and helped each other kill hogs. Most of the meat was preserved for later use. Sausage was made and ham and shoulders were "cured." The curing of the meat gave it a delightful taste and aroma when it was cooked in the old, black iron skillets.

The farmers always helped each other when sickness occurred. Their wives took turns caring for the sick so the farmer could keep his crops worked out. If a farmer himself were sick for a period of time, his neighbors would come together and do whatever work needed to be done. Whenever a house or a barn burned the neighbors came together and built a new one.

Building a new home for a neighbor was called a houseraising. The new home would be built with sweat, neighborliness, and love.

Corn shuckings were events that delighted all the farm families. After a farmer had gathered his corn and piled it in front of his crib, he would invite his neighbors in for a corn shucking. After the corn was shucked and thrown into the crib, the boys would play in the large pile of the shucks until supper time. After supper, they would all sit around the fire and enjoyed a time of talking, singing, and telling tall tales. Late at night, after their visit was over, everyone returned to their homes. After a night's rest the dawning of a new day meant another day of hard work.

Around 1833 the first cotton gin and wheat thresh were brought into the county.

The settlers were prosperous for awhile. Then in 1861 came the War Between the States. The sons of the "Free State of Carroll" took up arms for the Confederacy, although the county had voted against secession.

After the hardships of the war, the county settled down to an era of hard work and domesticity. The county grew steadily in population and wealth. Advancement was quite regular and uniform. Farmers improved rapidly until Carroll County stood paramount among agricultural counties of the state.

The only decade of economic and cultural lag was from 1860 to 1870, the miserable era of civil strife.

After the close of the Civil War in 1865, reconstruction of the South began. The railroads that had been destroyed were rebuilt. Atlanta built again on the original site where only charred timbers and ashes lay. Many new factories were built in Atlanta; thus a need for large quantities of coal and iron was pressing if the city was to become an industrial center.

For a number of years, Atlanta, formerly Marthasville, tried unsuccessfully to build a railroad to the nearby inexhaustible coal fields of Alabama. The desire of the city to build a railroad westward ultimately came to be and resulted in the towns of Temple and Bremen coming into existence.

CHAPTER IV

PIONEERS

The following biographical sketches of Temple men appeared in *Memoirs of Georgia*, Volume 1, 1895. They are presented here as a tribute to them and all the early settlers which they represent. Furthermore, the colorful life stories which were written during their lifetimes serve to authenticate the times.

Z.T. ADAMS, farmer, Temple, Carroll Co., Ga., son of Absalom and Elizabeth (Reid) Adams, was born in Carroll County in 1845. His grandparents, Adams, were Virginians, and moved thence to Tennessee, whence they subsequently came to Carroll County, where they died. Mr. Adams' father came from Tennessee to Georgia and settled in Carroll County in 1829, where he cleared a farm. He was a soldier in the Indian war of 1838. His great-grandfather on his mother's side, Reid, was a soldier in the war of 1812, during which he was shot in the stomach, the ball passing through the body. A silk handkerchief was drawn through the orifice afterward and he recovered and lived many years. His maternal grandparents, Reid, were early settlers in this part of the state. Mr. Adams was reared on the farm and received a common country school education. Being too young to enter the Confederate service, he enlisted, in 1863, in Company F (Capt. Long), Georgia regiment, state troops. Mr. Adams was married in 1864 to Miss Rebecca C. Coleman, daughter of W.A. and Sarah Ann (Barnes) Coleman, old settlers of this part of the state. When he was married he had nothing – was very poor. He has always been a plain farmer; has now a nice improved farm of nearly 200 acres with a comfortable house on it, within the corporate limits of Temple. Mr. and Mrs. Adams have six children born to them: William M., Henry T., a teacher in Texas, David N., Gilbert E., Z.T., and Bessie. Himself and wife are devoted and exemplary members of the Missionary Baptist Church.

MOSES J. BAXTER, farmer, Temple, Carroll Co., Ga., son of John and Elizabeth (Stripling) Baxter, was born in Monroe County, Ga., in 1828. His paternal grandparents were John and Nancy (Dowdy) Baxter. His grandfather was born in England, and came to this country after the Revolutionary War. He settled first in Virginia, afterward moved to North Carolina, and finally came all the way from North Carolina to Georgia in an ox-cart, and settled in the woods in Monroe County – among its pioneers. He followed farming all his life. He was a soldier of the War of 1812, and during his service had a remarkable experience with a wound. The ball went entirely through his body, and a silk handkerchief was drawn through the orifice, yet he recovered and lived many years in excellent health afterward. Mr. Baxter's father was born in 1807, and came to Georgia when a small boy with his father, who came to Carroll County in 1828; the subject of this sketch was an infant at the time, and the unconscious subject of a thrilling incident. The trip had been made in ox-carts, and when they reached the Chattahoochee River a nurse insisted on taking the baby in her arms. When the boat reached the opposite bank, the steers became scared and balked, and the nurse jumped overboard with our subject in her arms. When she arose to the surface his father caught and drew them out. His father was a soldier in the Indian War of 1836; and, also, was a member of the Methodist church. His maternal grandparents, John and Mary Stripling, were among the early settlers of Monroe County. Mr. Baxter was reared on the farm in Carroll County, and the very limited education he received was at the old time dirt floor log house, with

Mr. and Mrs. Moses J. Baxter

its unsatisfactory accompaniments. In 1862 he enlisted in Company F, Cobb's legion, and went to the front. But he was soon taken sick and was sent to Richmond, where he remained many months, and when he had apparently recovered he returned to the army. It was not long before he was again prostrated, and, this time, came home on a furlough – he was at home at the time of surrender. Like thousands of others, the war left him stripped of everything; but like them, he went bravely to work, impaired in health as he was, to build up. By dint of hard work and close management he has a fine, large farm, well improved, with nice dwelling and substantial out buildings, half a mile from Temple; and commands the respect of all who know him. Mr. Baxter was married in 1852 to Miss Sarah J., daughter of James and Elizabeth (Baskin) Stripling, early settlers, by whom he has had eight children: William A., N.N., James D., Robert A., John M., Geo. Ann Florence, Frances, and Martha. Mr. Baxter is a master Mason and himself and wife are members of the Methodist church.

JAMES P. GRIFFIN, merchant, Temple, Carroll Co., son of Charles W. and Sarah (New) Griffin, was born in DeKalb County in 1838. His paternal grandparent, James P. Griffin, was a native of South Carolina, came to Georgia in 1818, and settled in what is now DeKalb County. At that time they had to tramp their wheat out on the floor. He was a soldier in the War of 1812. Mr. Griffin's father was born in Abbeville district, S.C., in 1811, came to Georgia with his parents when he was seven years old, and was reared on the farm originally settled. He followed farming all his life, was a soldier in the Indian War of 1836, and was a member of the Methodist church. His maternal grandparent, Joel New, was a native of South Carolina and among the early settlers of DeKalb County. Mr. Griffin was reared on a farm in rural Carroll County, where he went with the family when he was eight years old. His father being a poor man, and the eldest boy of eleven children, had to work very hard, and was almost entirely deprived of the school advantages he yearned for. Oftentimes, too, he had to plow through briar patches and his feet would get so badly torn he could hardly walk. After he became of age he "boarded himself" and went to school. In 1862 he enlisted in Company E (Capt. Blalock), First Georgia cavalry, and during the war was in many hard-fought battles, among them Richmond, Ky., Wheeler's Gap, Murfreesboro, Chickamauga, Resaca, and then thence to Atlanta and on to Macon. At the time of surrender he was at Greensborough, N.C. He was in numerous minor engagements, and during his service had several horses shot out from under him, but was so fortunate as to escape being wounded or captured. A part of the time he acted as orderly-sergeant. After the war Mr. Griffin worked a farm at fifty cents a day and taught school. Struggling on, working hard, and saving his money, he at last came into the ownership of a 500 acre farm of good land, and well improved. In 1881 he engaged in a general merchandising business at Temple, where he has built up a good and profitable trade and has made and is making money. For six years he served as justice of the peace. Intelligent, industrious, and economical, in connection with energy and judicious enterprise, it may be expected his achieved success will be far exceeded by that of the future. Mr. Griffin was married in 1868 to Miss Sarah A. Adams – born and reared in Carroll County – daughter of Absalom and Elizabeth (Reid) Adams, by whom he has had seven children: Joseph, Ryburn, M.E., Bettie M., Lewis, Ella, and Claudie. Mr.Griffin is a member of the Masonic fraternity, and himself and wife and all the children except the baby are members of the Methodist Church.

HENRY F. CRAWFORD, farmer, Temple, Carroll Co., Ga., son of Gallant and Katie Crawford, was born in what is now Spalding County in 1846. His paternal grandfather, William Crawford, was a native Virginian, came to Georgia in ox-carts in 1810, and settled in the woods. He was a soldier of the War of 1812. Mr. Crawford's father was born in what is now Henry County, in 1816, and was reared a farmer, and followed farming all his life. He was a soldier in the Indian War of 1836. His maternal grandparents were among the first settlers and wealthy citizens of that part of the state. Mr. Crawford was reared on the farm and had to work hard, and so had to be content with a very limited education. In 1864 he enlisted in company F (Capt. Thomas), Phillips' legion, and, although his service was not lengthy, it was rough and arduous. He participated in the Bellfield creek rail – three days' fighting – the battle of Petersburg, and the stirring events of the closing scenes of the war. He was in the engagement of Orangeburg, S.C., and Salisbury, N.C. and was at Charlotte, N.C. at the time of the surrender. After the war he came home and engaged in farming. In 1870, Mr. Crawford was married to Miss Nancy, daughter of John and Eliza (Weidner) Lee. Mr. Lee, her father, was born in Kentucky in 1818, and when seventeen years of age ran away from home and came to Georgia with some hog drivers, and never returned. Having fine business capacity, and being a shrewd trader, he became very rich, but the war about ruined him. When Mr. Crawford married he was very poor, but not discouraged, and his wife provided a helpmeet, indeed; she worked with him in the field during the day, and at night spun and wove the cloth and made the clothing for the family. Thus they worked together and struggled on as plain farmers, until now he has a good 200-acre farm and comfortable home where he lives, and nearby a 250-acre tract of choice land. To them six children have been born: Alice, wife of Cas Cantrell; Robert, Frank, William H., Rilla, and O.V. Mr. and Mrs. Crawford are members of the Missionary Baptist

Church, content with their success in life, and happy in the consciousness of having the confidence and esteem of their neighbors.

B. J. McCAIN, merchant, Temple, Carroll Co., Ga., son of William B. and Margaret N. (McCain) McCain, was born in Troup County in 1843. His grandparent, Hugh McCain, was a native of North Carolina and was a soldier in the Revolutionary war. His parents were born in North Carolina, came to Georgia and settled in Troup County in 1840, where his father cleared a farm and built for himself two mills, merchant and saw mill. His maternal grandparents, Joe and Margaret (Moore) McCain, were also born in North Carolina. Mr. McCain was reared on the farm and his early education was obtained at a country school. In 1863 he enlisted in Company F (Capt. B.F. Long), cavalry, with which he served six months. He then enlisted in Company F (Capt. George Austin), Georgia state troops, with which he remained until the close of the war, and of which he was a corporal. He was in two battles, both fought at Coosahatchie, and at the surrender he stacked arms at Albany, Ga. After the war he returned to the farm, but in 1868 he attended school in Carrollton. The next year he worked on the farm, and the one following he attended a private school for four months. In 1871 he finished his preparatory commercial education by attending Moore's Business University at Atlanta. In August, 1872, he engaged as a clerk with J. C. Carter with whom he remained four years. After that he entered into partnership with Gus Smythe, but at the end of fifteen months he sold out to his partner and formed a new partnership with L. P. Barnes. Twelve months after he retired from this business, and with George and John McGahee and I. Y. Sawtell organized the Atlanta Wild Land Company. He remained in this company ten months, and then, in the fall of 1878, located in Simsville, Ga., and engaged in a general merchandise business in which he was satisfactorily successful. In 1882 he closed out in Simsville and permanently settled in Temple, where he is now, and where he has built a large and profitable trade, and is a leading business man and citizen of that part of the county. In 1875 Mr. McCain was married to Miss Tallulah V., daughter of Maj. D. A. and Nancy W. (Collier) Cook, of Atlanta, by whom he has one child surviving, Ida Tallulah. They have an adopted son, William B. Mr. McCain is a master Mason and he and his family are members of the Methodist church. He exerts a well-earned influence in the community and county.

WILLIAM M. SPENCE, farmer, Carrollton, Carroll Co., Ga., {Abilene vicinity} son of Hiram and Angeline (Cheney) Spence, was born in Morgan County, Ga., in 1845. His paternal grandparents, George and Mary (Knight) Spence, were born in Maryland, came to Georgia in ox-carts in 1798 and settled in the woods in what is now Morgan County. He was a delegate to the secession convention, served many years as a justice of the peace and lived to be a very old man. Mr. Spence's parents were born in Morgan County, his father in 1821, and removed to Carroll County in 1847, settling in the woods and clearing for a farm the place where Mr. Spence now lives. He was a justice of the peace for many years. During the war he served in the state militia and served in the defense of Atlanta. Both parents were members of the Primitive Baptist Church and were much esteemed by their neighbors. The parents of his mother, Thomas and Lucy Cheney, were born in Maryland and came to Georgia in 1798. They ranked among the best people in every respect. Mr. Spence was reared on the farm where he now lives, and taught by his mother, he learned his A B C's out of the old family Bible. The he attended school in a log cabin in the woods, with dirt floor, seats made of slabs and the chimney of sticks and mud, with square holes cut through the sides for windows. In March, 1864, he enlisted in Company K, Second Georgia regiment, known as state line troops and after the Confederate army entered Georgia, served under Gens. Johnston and Hood. After the war he resumed farming, at which he has prospered and placed himself in comfortable circumstances. Mr. Spence was married in 1868 to Miss Delphia McPherson (born in Carroll County), daughter of Elijah and Sarah McPherson, who migrated from Tennessee to Georgia and were among the early settlers of the county. To them nine children have been born: Leon, Ella, Ida, Cora, William, Newton, Albert, Mary, and Ivey. Mr. Spence is regarded as one of the county's most substantial and reliable citizens, and is highly respected by all who know him. Mrs. Spence is a member of the Primitive Baptist Church.

The following sketches appeared in *Georgia*, Volume I, Edited by Gov. Allen D. Chandler and Gen. Clement A. Evans, Published in Atlanta by the State Historical Association, 1906.

BASKIN, CHARLES L., M.D. – Carroll County has its full quota of skilled and successful physicians and surgeons and among the number is Dr. Charles L. Baskin, who is a representative of old and honored families of that section of the state and who enjoys unqualified popularity in his native county. He was born in Carroll County, Jan. 27, 1869, a son of Thomas W. and Hattie (Chandler) Baskin, both natives of that county, where the respective families were early established. Thomas W. Baskin was born at Hickory Level, Feb. 19, 1845, a son of Rev. James Baskin, a clergyman of the Methodist Episcopal church who came from South Carolina to Georgia in 1826, settled at Hickory Level and became one of the extensive land-owners in Carroll County. Thomas W. Baskin was a loyal soldier of the Confederacy during the Civil War, as a member of the Nineteenth Georgia infantry. His vocation in life was that of farming and he was one of the honored and influential citizens of Carroll County, where he died in 1879. His wife was born in Carrollton, where she still maintains her home, was a daughter of Thomas Chandler, who was one of the first settlers of that place, having located there about 1825. He was an able lawyer and practiced his profession with marked success. He effected a treaty between a number of white settlers and the Indians and for his service was given a considerable body of land, where Carrollton now stands. He was a man of prominence and influence, active in public affairs, frequently served as a delegate to state conventions of his political party and stood high in the esteem of all who knew him. Dr. Charles L. Baskin secured his early educational training in the public schools of Carrollton, and was then matriculated in the Atlanta College of Physicians and Surgeons, in which excellent institution he was graduated in April, 1895, with the degree of Doctor of Medicine. He forthwith opened an office in Temple, where he has since been engaged in active practice and where he has met with unequivocal success in his chosen profession. He is identified with the Medical Association of Georgia and with the Carroll County medical society; is local surgeon for the Southern railway; is president of the Temple board of health and also president of the board of education of the town. In politics he is a stanch Democrat; his religious faith is that of the Baptist church, of which his wife also is a member; and is affiliated with the local lodge and chapter of the Masonic fraternity. On Dec.18, 1890, Doctor Baskin was united in marriage to Miss Martha Connell, daughter of Thomas and Martha (Arnold) Connell, of Carroll County. She was summoned to the life eternal on Dec. 2, 1903, and is survived by three children, - Todd, Edwin and Hattie. On Jan.14, 1906, Doctor Baskin married Miss Kate Connell, a sister of his first wife.

ENTERKIN, WARNER A., an influential and honored citizen and prominent business man of the thriving town of Temple, Carroll County, has been closely identified with the upbuilding of the place and is one of its most loyal and enterprising citizens. He was born in Douglas County, Ga., October 20, 1859, and is a son of David F. and Mary (Leathers) Enterkin, the former of whom was born in North Carolina and the latter in Georgia. The mother died in 1861 and the father, who has been a farmer all his life, still continues to reside in Douglas County. His father, David Enterkin, was a soldier in the Seminole Indian War. The educational advantages of the subject of this sketch were those afforded by the schools of his native county, and at the age of twenty years he engaged in farming on his own responsibility. A year later, however, he secured a position as clerk in a general store of Douglasville, where he remained thus engaged for three years. In 1882 he took up his residence in Temple, where he became a member of the firm of Griffin & Enterkin, engaged in the general merchandise business, the partnership continuing until 1895, when Mr. Enterkin became sole proprietor of the business, which he has since continued most successfully, having one of the largest and best equipped stores in the town and commanding a representative patronage. He also gives special attention to handling cotton and fertilizers, is a member of the board of directors of the Temple Banking Company, and is the owner of a well improved plantation in Carroll County. When he located in Temple the village had a population of about fifty persons and there were only two stores. The place now has 400 inhabitants and is a thriving and attractive village. Mr. Enterkin has shown a public spirited interest in his home town and county and has been a liberal supporter of all measures and enterprises tending to advance the general welfare and material upbuilding of Temple. As a citizen he commands the unqualified esteem and confidence of the community, his name being a synonym of integrity and honor. He is aligned as a stanch supporter of the cause of the Democratic party and has served several terms as a member of the village council. He is a member of the local lodge of Free and Accepted Masons, and both he and his wife are zealous members of the Methodist Episcopal Church South. On Nov.12, 1885, Mr. Enterkin was united in marriage to Miss Margaret Dempsey, daughter of Clark and Elizabeth (Adams) Dempsey, of Carroll County, and of their six children all are living but the second, Dewitt B., who died at the age of 2 years. The names of the others are as follows: Emmett B., Earl, Ernest, Jewel and Ruby.

CHAPTER V

EARLY SETTLEMENTS

Courtesy, Mrs. Jesse Hamrick

Artist Jack Ashmore's Interpretation of Buckhorn Tavern

In 1833, when the bear, wolf, and catamount still roamed the dense forest of northwestern Carroll County, a large, double, log house was built by an early settler. William West was the first occupant and kept open house there for many years. A wide, open entry or dog trot ran through the middle of the house. Along this entry hung several huge deer antlers. The place became known as Buckhorn Tavern because of the display of the horns. The cabin was built on the crest of a red hill and became a famous hostelry on the stagecoach route between Marthasville and Jacksonville, Alabama.

The house, along with several hundred acres of forest-covered land, was later bought by Isaac E. Cobb. Cobb was an energetic huntsman and when he returned from his kills of wolf, deer, and bear, he nailed the horns of the buck on trees, under the eaves of the house, and along the entry. The travelers used these as hangers for their hats, coats, and saddle bags. The horns also served as hay racks in the stables.

The stagecoaches that stopped at the tavern with weary travelers were drawn by four and sometimes six horses. The seating capacity on the coaches was from eight to ten with the baggage piled on top.

It is said that when a stage was about a mile from the tavern, the driver would sound a blast on a hunting horn for each passenger he carried, and by the time it arrived the table was set for the exact number of guests. This often repeated story is perhaps true as there is corroboration in historical accounts concerning the sounding of horns at Georgia stagecoach stops. From the *Cyclopedia of Georgia* published in 1906: "Few men are now living who are old enough to remember the old coaching days in all their glory; the sound of the horn to announce the arrival of the stage; the sharp crack of the driver's whip as he proudly flourished the lash over the "leaders;" the open-mouthed wonder of the small boy as the lumbering vehicle drew up to the station…another blast of the horn" (upon departure).

Attendants took care of the stage, and the horses were fed and watered or fresh horses were hitched up and ready to go by the time dinner was finished. If guests spent the night, they slept in two large rooms – ladies on the ground floor and men in the attic.

On September 16, 1856, a post office was established at Buckhorn Tavern, thereby becoming Buck Horn, Georgia. The first postmaster was Joseph L. Hart. The post office was discontinued in 1857.

During the Civil War, Confederate soldiers camped around the tavern and were extended hospitality by the innkeeper.

John M. Walker purchased the farm from the Cobb estate. Then in 1925, the old log cabin was bought by J.P. Carnes, a section foreman for the Southern Railroad and great-grandfather of Mark and Scott Holder. He weatherboarded the old house and painted it white. Tenant farmers lived there.

Part of the original foundation and framework, held together with wooden pins, still stood as the oldest structure in Carroll County until 2001 when it was dismantled. The old hostelry one and one-half miles east of Temple could be seen from Highway 78. The original road was on the opposite side of the building from the location of the present highway. In 1958, the tavern and farm were bought from the Carnes estate by Leon Lee of Villa Rica who developed the land into a cattle farm.

RINGER'S CROSS ROADS. Many years before the Civil War a log cabin marked the spot of Ringer's Cross Roads. This place was later called Temple. Here the Carrollton-Cedartown and the Atlanta-Jacksonville roads crossed. Ringer's Cross Roads was named for an early settler, Benjamin F. Ringer.

There were no business houses there, but several good farms had been established and crops were grown in the fertile gray and red soil. Several churches and one-room schools were nearby in the countryside.

Some of the settlers before 1860 were Rev. William Brooks, Rev. Mr. Riggs, David Bryant, Absalom Adams, George Davis, Joe Webster, the Cartwrights, Crockets, Jimmie Taylor, Jesse Kinney, and Mat Lovell.

A few miles north of Ringer's Cross Roads was the trail which separated the Creek Indian Nation from the Cherokees.

SIMSVILLE. About three miles southeast of Ringer's Cross Roads there was a thriving settlement known as Simsville. The main crops grown there were cotton and corn, and at one time there were four cotton gins. Simsville was a flourishing community for a number of years before the railroad was built through Ringer's Cross Roads. Simsville had a population of about 200.

A post office was established on July 20, 1876, with George W. Autry as the first postmaster. B.J. McCain also served as postmaster there. The post office, which received mail once a week, was discontinued in 1883.

Simsville had two doctors: James F. Brooks and Richard L. Rowe. Dr. Rowe was one of the county's two representatives to the State Constitutional Convention of 1877.

Cotton gins were operated by J. P. Griffin, J. M. Street, H. McPherson, and Hill Brothers. Sawmills and grist mills were run by James Chance and J. P. Griffin. Williams Mill was also located there. A. L. Waddell operated a flour mill.

The Justices Court Ground of the old Sixth District was located at Simsville at Sharp and Cheney's store. An old man and his wife were always there in a covered, one-steer wagon with ginger cakes, "simmon beer," and apple cider to sell. The cakes sold for a "thrip" as did cider and beer per cup. A "thrip" was a small, silver five-cent piece.

The nearest railroad was twelve miles southward at Carrollton. From that point, the farmers shipped their cotton to market. They also traded with the merchants there whose wares were brought from Atlanta by wagon train.

In the area stood the Old Bethel Primitive Baptist Church. It was made of logs and had no steeple. Though the church was most rustic in appearance, the farmers gathered, the old elder rode up, tied his horse to a sapling, and preached the gospel as he saw it. The singing of the old hymns could be heard afar as the melodious notes pealed through the quiet countryside.

The old church is gone, but the old cemetery, a placid reminder of days long ago, can still be seen today. This cemetery is the final resting place of Isaac E. Cobb, who was a member of the state Legislature in the 1830s and 1840s. He was the sheriff of the county for three consecutive terms. He was also the distinguished host of Buckhorn Tavern. The cemetery is located on Bar J Road at S Red Oak Way.

CHAPTER VI

GEORGIA PACIFIC RAILROAD

As early as 1870, during Reconstruction days, state officials commenced building the Georgia Western Railroad from Atlanta to the Alabama coal fields. This road was to be routed through Douglasville and Carrollton. The grading as far as Douglasville was largely completed. Even though the road was state supported, northern capital was also involved. Northern capitalists, often derisively called carpetbaggers during this era, were frequently met with distrust. This too was the case with the effort to build the Georgia Western. The resulting conflicts stopped construction and the plan was abandoned.

Many times for the next ten years attempts were made to build this road. The railroad was reorganized time and time again. Each time the plan failed for one reason or another. Much of the time the building of the road existed only as a dormant dream. It seemed that Atlanta would never have direct access to the much needed iron and coal of Alabama. However, cheap coal was a must if Atlanta was to become the great city that it desired to be. It was proposed, as it had been many times before, that the Georgia Western be built to the sources of iron and coal. Once again the proposal failed.

In May of 1880, John B. Gordon resigned from the United States Senate and took a position with the Louisville and Nashville railroad as its general counsel. Soon he began the task of securing the charter of the Georgia Western Railroad from the L. and N. and consolidating it with the other lines to form the Georgia Pacific Railway Company.

Then on December 31, 1881, after months of organizing, John B. Gordon and his brothers, E.C. and Walter Gordon, Governor A.H. Colquitt and other stockholders met at the Relay House in Birmingham to incorporate the Georgia Pacific Railway Company. The well capitalized Richmond and Danville Syndicate took in the Georgia Pacific. Finally, a line was to be built from Atlanta to Birmingham and on to the Mississippi River. The Georgia Pacific was incorporated especially for this purpose. Gordon was the first president of the new company. He held this position of leadership until he resigned in 1883. Robert H. Temple was Chief Engineer.

Construction of the line was to be through Carrollton as originally planned some ten years before. In January of 1882, a Gordon representative met with a group of Carrollton citizens at the courthouse to discuss the building of the new road. To say the least, the meeting did not prove to be successful. As a result, Gordon immediately changed the proposed route of the road. He decided to build it through the northern part of the county.

Construction of the Georgia Pacific Railroad started almost immediately. Construction was pushed rapidly and within a year a vast new trade area was opened up to Atlanta. Farmers began shipping their cotton and other products to Atlanta as soon as the railroad reached their section of the state.

On November 16, 1883, at 10 p.m., the last spike was driven at Cave Creek Tunnel, Alabama, thus completing the connection between Atlanta and Birmingham by the Georgia Pacific Railroad.

As though the newly-laid rails of steel were magnetic, people were attracted from far and near. As the settlers gathered along the tracks, they built wood-frame store houses, dwellings, churches, and schools. Lively new towns were born. One of them was Temple, on the site of Ringer's Cross Roads. Out of sparsely settled northwestern Carroll County where the narrow dirt road from

Carrollton to Cedartown crossed the road running west to Jacksonville and eastward to Atlanta, the town of Temple had its beginning.

The town of Temple is a by-product of the stamina and ingenuity of John B. Gordon when he organized, incorporated, and built the Georgia Pacific railroad through this place.

To show their appreciation to Gordon for making their coveted railroad a reality, a banquet was given in his honor by prominent Atlanta merchants, manufacturers, capitalists, and professional men.

Gordon served in the U.S. Senate from 1873 to 1880 when he resigned to incorporate the Georgia Pacific. In 1886, he became Governor of Georgia and was elected again in 1888. A statue of the man who caused life to be breathed into this place stands on the capitol grounds – brave, staunch, and proud.

Artist E.T. Crisp's Interpretation of the First Locomotive Through Temple

CHAPTER VII

TEMPLE

The fall of 1881 was not unlike the ones of previous years at this place known as Ringer's Cross Roads, named for Benjamin F. Ringer who settled there in 1862.

Farmers of the area were busy gathering their crops before cold weather. The fleecy, white cotton was being picked by the farm families and then hauled by wagons to nearby Simsville to be ginned. Wheat and corn were also carried to the same thriving community to be ground into flour and meal. Preparations were made for the winter's supply of food because soon the rains and bitter cold weather would render the narrow, dirt roads almost impassable.

After the cotton was ginned, the farmers turned their wagons southward and traveled to Carrollton, the nearest railroad town. The cotton was sold and supplies bought from the Carrollton merchants whose stores were nestled around the square of the county seat. Trading was also done at Simsville; two general stores were located there as well as a post office in the store of B.J. McCain. Farmers living north of the crossroads sometimes traveled to Matt Lovell's store at Mt. Carmel to buy coffee, sugar, and other things they could not produce at home.

No business was done at Ringer's Cross Roads. Only a single log cabin marked the spot. The countryside was quiet and serene. Much of the land was covered in virgin forest.

The earth was studded with giant trees of oak, hickory, and pine. Their fallen leaves and twigs made a thick, brown carpet on the earth's floor. Wild deer, turkey, opossum, and raccoon abounded in the area. They were disturbed only occasionally by the few early settlers when they hunted for wild game. The clear, sparkling streams were filled with fish. The panther and the howl of the wolf could be heard at night when all was still and quiet. The owl and whippoorwill also broke the silence of the night when they gave their lonesome calls.

The early settlers worshiped at Asbury Chapel Methodist Church which was located just northwest of the crossroads, or at Mt. Carmel which was a few miles farther north. Some attended the Old Bethel Primitive Baptist Church at Simsville while others traveled by wagon to New Bethel Baptist on Carrollton Road.

A few, small one-room schools were scattered about which offered the three R's and the hickory stick for about three months each year. School was sometimes housed in a church or a farmer's home. Farming activities and distance kept many children from attending regularly. Some hardly attended at all and grew up with very little schooling.

Rail-splitting was an important activity during the winter months. After the trees were felled and split, the wooden rails were laid in a crisscross fashion to keep swine, sheep and cattle out of the fields. There were no fence laws so the farmers' livestock roamed the countryside feeding off the lush grass and fruits of the forest trees.

The quiet, isolated countryside now stood in the very doorway of a drastic change. For months the farm families of the area had been hearing rumors that a railroad was to be built from Atlanta to Birmingham. However, they had been hearing this rumor off and on for years, and it had yet to become a reality. Then, too, the proposed route had always been through Carrollton which would not make too much of an impact on Ringer's Cross Roads.

Then, toward the end of 1881, the railroad rumor took on new life and quite a stir was in evidence at the crossroads. A new railroad company had been organized according to an Atlanta newspaper, and General John B. Gordon, president of the road, seemed to be determined that rails of steel would, once again, penetrate Carroll County. A fact even more profound was his decision to build the new road through Ringer's Cross Roads and onward to the coal fields and iron beds of Alabama. It would extend even farther and penetrate the cotton belt of Mississippi. The road was to be built by the Richmond and Danville Extension Company.

The new railroad would bring coal, iron, and farm products to Atlanta. These products would strengthen and expand the businesses and industries that had been destroyed when Sherman and his troops set the city aflame on their march to the sea.

The first surveyors soon arrived and marked the trees to reveal the exact route the steel rails would take. The giant trees, which had stood for so many years, would soon yield to the ax and crash to the ground in thunderous roars.

The famous Cotton Exposition of 1881 opened in the fall at Atlanta's Oglethorpe Park. On November 18, from this site, General and Mrs. Gordon walked across a field and joined a group of railroad construction men who were working on the roadbed of the new railroad. Gordon was handed a huge hammer with which he enthusiastically drove the first spike. The "iron horse" was finally on its way toward northern Carroll.

A new, bustling railroad town was envisioned by business men of Carroll and surrounding counties. The crossroads soon became quite a lively spot as prospective merchants, millers, ginners, sawmillers, and carpenters arrived to look over the land which would be suitable for their enterprises.

As the prospectors looked over the site of the new town, they could hear blasting in the distance. The blasts of the dynamite clearing the road's path seemed to be continually announcing that the railroad was on its way.

In January 1882, Doctors James F. Brooks, Richard L. Rowe of Simsville and James P. Griffin of the same community began building the first store on the south side of the proposed railroad tracks. By early spring, Griffin and his brother Thomas offered general merchandise to the railroad construction men and farm families who lived nearby. The simple, wood-frame building soon became the center of activity. Railroad and farm news was freely shared as the newly-arrived railroad men, other newcomers, and the local farmers met here.

One of the first things the citizens of the new town did was to secure a post office. The office was opened on April 24, 1882, in Griffin Brothers store with James H. Allen as postmaster. Legend has it that when it was time to name the new post office, a group of men were pondering over a name when the Chief Civil Engineer of the railroad spoke up and remarked, "Why not name it for me?" This they did: they named the new town Temple, in honor of Major Robert Henry Temple, a Civil War veteran from Virginia.

Farmers experienced quite a measure of prosperity during the summer of 1882. Crops in the area were extremely good. However, farmers found it difficult to hire farm laborers since most of them had gone to work for the railroad. They were making more money than they had ever made on the farms.

Farmers were happy over the price of land. It was bringing as much as $23 per acre near the post office.

In May 1882, the railroad reached Douglasville and the first bale of cotton was shipped from Douglasville via the new road.

During the summer, the rhythmic ring of iron spikes being driven into crossties constantly reminded everyone that Temple, a new railroad town, had been born.

In mid-August, the first "iron horse," with smoke billowing from its smokestack, shattered the quietness of the settlement as it thundered into town. Temple now had good transportation by which to ship its cotton to market. The steam locomotives opened the curtains to the east and west, and the town stood on the threshold of a boom. The people now had a means of travel for business purposes, as well as for pleasure.

TEMPLE! FINE LOTS. What follows is reproduced from the poster announcing the sale at auction of town lots. The town of Temple begins amid great fanfare!

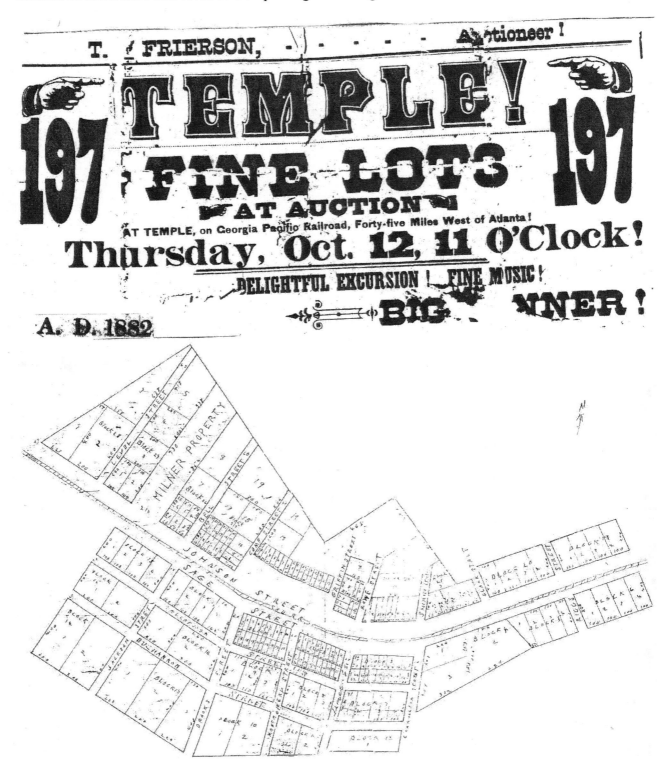

The remainder of the poster reads as follows:

The above plat represents the town of Temple, situated on the Georgia Pacific Railroad, 45 miles west of Atlanta, in Carroll County, Ga. Temple is on a beautiful, elevated plateau, fronting nicely to the railroad and streets. Some of the lots are on open ground, but most of them are covered with fine, original oak and hickory trees. Temple is a most beautiful and attractive location for a town, and cannot fail to become a very important place. It is in the midst of a most prosperous and densely populated community; it is surrounded for many miles by a splendid agricultural country - one of the best in Georgia - which is almost as thickly settled as Ireland with independent and wealthy farmers, from whom the new town will receive a healthy support. Its high and aired position renders it exceeding healthful and pleasant as a residence place, and will in the future make it a popular health and pleasure resort. The great abundance and variety of country produce yielded annually by the fertile farms for many miles around, will at once make Temple an important commercial point, and cause it to grow readily in size and importance. Four main, public highways from Carrollton to Cedartown and Rome, and from Atlanta to Jacksonville and Birmingham, Ala., intersect right in the heart of Temple, and the great travel on these thoroughfares must pass into and through the town and contribute to its importance as a central point for all the country around. The Georgia Pacific Railroad runs centrally through the town, thus giving it transportation facilities, and direct communication and connection with an immense scope of territory, embracing several States. Another railroad, from Rome to Carrollton and Bowdon, will soon be built, and will cross the Georgia Pacific Railroad at Temple, and make it a place to grow rapidly. {note: This railroad was built through Bremen instead.} The corporators of the new railroad, composed of Gen. Gordon, Gov. Colquitt, Maj. Temple, Col. Johnston and others, have already given notice of application for charter to next Legislature. The nearest town to Temple is 8 miles, next 12 miles, and next 20 miles, so that there is nothing to divert the immense supply of produce and trade of the rich country around from Temple, and it is obliged to be a very fine business point. The Georgia Pacific depot, a large and handsome structure, is nearly completed, and stands about the center of Temple, and there is a side track already built, 1200 feet long. The officials of the Georgia Pacific Railroad, and all who are familiar with the road and the towns along the line, and the country around them, are united in the opinion that Temple is the most important point on the railroad from Atlanta to Anniston, Ala. All are agreed that Temple is destined to be the largest, most popular and important town on the road. The opinions of such men are reliable, because they are well informed: and all who wish to secure fine country homes, or make safe and profitable investments, or secure good business stands, where trade will be lively and money easily made, and where business can be built up and increased with the town, should not neglect this rare opportunity. Before long accommodation trains will be run on this road for benefit of city people who have village and country homes along the line.

A special train will leave the Carshead at 7 o'clock, with ample room for all. Round trip fare, including dinner, as follows: from Atlanta, $1.25; Mableton, $1.00; Austell, 85cts.; Salt Springs, 75 cts.; Douglasville, 65 cts.; Winns, 50 cts.; Villa Rica 25 cts.; (Missing) Cornet Band will discourse good music from 6 to 7 o'clock at the Carshead and during the day. A good, big, old fashioned country barbecue will be served in abundance for all, and in the shady grove on the ground. Bill of Fare as follows: barbecued shotes, mutton, kid and beef; roast beef and fowls; boiled ham; fried chicken, bread, potatoes; vegetables in variety; cakes, pies, fruits etc. No charge for dinner nor anything except railroad fare, which is very low for such a pleasant trip, good dinner and enjoyable recreation. All who can possibly enjoy this pleasant trip over the new road and through a new country, should be sure to do so, and no one will regret it. Combine business and pleasure, and secure some of the fine lots to be sold, and it will pay you.....

A. D. 1882

Out of sparsely settled northwestern Carroll County this place was surveyed and platted. On October 12, 1882, a big auction was held to sell town lots. A special train brought prospective buyers from Atlanta. People came from all around to enjoy the barbecue dinner and to listen to an Atlanta brass band. The prospective lot buyers were filled with excitement and anticipation as they vied for the choice lots along the railroad tracks. This was the first, big social event for the bustling, new village. The new depot was under construction in October as well. The building, a 27 by 70 feet wooden structure, was welcomed by the residents. It became quite a social center as people gathered to see who was arriving or leaving town. The mail trains were awaited anxiously to see if a letter had arrived from a faraway friend or relative. The depot was situated just west of downtown and Montgomery Street, between the main railroad track and the sidetrack.

The people who were already settled around Temple developed friendships with the engineers and others who supervised and constructed the railroad. Among them were Colonel Alex Montgomery, Colonel James, Major Johnston, and Major R. H. Temple (At this time less than two decades after the close of the Civil War, it was the custom to address veterans by their rank in the war). The local people regretted seeing them leave as they moved westward to complete the line.

For the next several months, trees were felled and sawmills hummed because lumber was needed to build the dwellings and stores that were in great demand. The sound of the saw and the hammer was heard in every direction. The new buildings were small and inexpensive, but they represented the faith the builders had in the future of the new town.

New families were moving in every few days. Some of them lived in the two boarding houses until their homes could be built.

The nearest settlement to Temple was Simsville, a thriving farming community some three miles to the southeast. There some 200 people lived; most of them were farmers. Many of them were drawn to the new developing town on the Georgia Pacific. James Brooks and Richard Rowe became the first doctors. They, too, moved from Simsville.

The townsmen planted sycamore trees in front of the new stores. The trees soon grew straight and tall and served as good hitching posts for the horses and mules. Also, it was not uncommon for the farmers to visit awhile in the shade before returning to their farms.

By the fall of 1883, Temple had ten dry goods and grocery stores, a millinery store, one livery stable almost completed, two blacksmith shops, and several excellent boarding houses.

Up to date, there had been about one thousand bales of cotton shipped by rail. The merchants had bought more than nine thousand chickens and twenty-nine thousand eggs from the farmers. The businesses thrived considering the stringency of the times. Excitement and optimism were high in the new bustling village.

The first settlers of Temple in the latter part of 1882 and early 1883 made immediate plans for providing schooling for their children and religious training for all citizenry.

A small, frame building called an academy in those days was built in early 1883 near where Buchanan Street joins the present First Baptist Church grounds. As was the custom then, the one-room academy served as a school during the weekdays and as a house of worship on Sundays. The very active Sabbath School met on Sunday afternoons with plenty of that "ole time religion" for everyone. P. I. Sewell, local hotel keeper, was the most capable song leader and superintendent. Music was a most important part of the Sunday afternoon services as men, women, and children blended their voices in praise to God. On Sunday mornings church services were held in the academy.

The Carroll County Sunday School Association, which had met annually since 1865, met in the various communities. This was quite an active organization and brought friend and kinfolk together from all over the county. These meetings also served as social gatherings. It was about the only time that friends and relatives living at a distance from one another were able to get together. They took meals and often spent the night in homes of the host community. It was about the only time that they could visit since the mode of travel and the demanding farming activities kept the farm families at home most of the time.

The town of Temple was incorporated by an act of the state legislature on August 28, 1883. On October 6 of that year, the first mayor and councilmen were elected. Uncle Jesse Kinney was elected mayor. J. T. Copeland, P. I. Sewell, A. H. Riggs, and Dr. J. F. Brooks were councilmen. One of their first duties was to appoint a marshal.

Music lessons were taught as early as 1885 when Mollie Rush of Atlanta taught in the home of John Copeland.

Early businesses included V. R. Davis and Cole Store, W. A. Enterkin, R. J. Holland and Son, Mr. Phillips, Griffin Brothers, Vines and Haynes Blacksmith Shop, Brooks and Rowe Drug Store, Riggs and Brooks Store, J. D. and A. H. Riggs, G. T. Williams and Dr. D. W. Dorsett Drug Store, Campbell and Bell Store, Williams Livery Stable, B. J. McCain, Williams and Mobley, Copeland, Baskin and Company, Barge and Company, and Mrs. B. J. McCain millinery.

The place of holding justice court in this district was moved from Simsville to Temple. The court house was on East Tallapoosa Street where the former warehouse of Thomas Hardware was located, just off Carrollton Street.

By the summer of 1884, lumber was hauled in to build a Methodist church on the site of the present building. The house was built sixty feet long and forty feet wide. The Baptists also built a wood-frame house of worship in 1884. This building was erected a few hundred feet west of the present Baptist church. It faced Buchanan Street.

Farmers could now raise better crops since guano and other supplies needed for farming were plentiful locally since being shipped in by rail. The area was developing very fast into a promising farming region and cotton market. Much of the land was fertile and the farmers were willing to work hard to produce good yields. Land was now selling from $10 to $20 per acre.

Clearing the land and tilling the soil was hard work. Life was simple but it was not easy. There were periods of drought when crops would not grow. Just as bad was when long rainy spells played havoc with the crops. The weeds would grow and choke the crops during long periods of rain. When the rains stopped, the farmer, his wife, and children had to work feverishly to rid the long rows of grass. Only then could the cotton and corn grow, mature and produce normal yields. The weather could make or break the farmer. This was something he could only wonder about, talk about, and pray about.

When farmers wanted to sell sheep or cattle, they drove the herd to the Gate City as Atlanta was called. This took about a week of the farmers' time. While in the Gate City, they bought a few supplies and simple surprise gifts for their families.

By late 1884, the wood-frame Methodist and Baptist churches had been completed. The members of Asbury Chapel Methodist Church, which was located about a mile northwest of Temple, chartered the new Methodist church and moved their memberships. The African-American families of the community built a church on West Johnson Street near the depot in 1888.

The small academy had one room. Here Temple's first schoolmaster, E. Lewis Connell, taught "readin, ritin, and rithmetic" to his young scholars. The older students helped the little ones with their reading and ciphering. Parents helped pay for their children's education. They built and maintained the academy and helped pay the meager salary of the schoolmaster. The school was open for two short sessions. The first was in the summer after the crops had been laid by and the other was after harvest time in late fall and winter. School was let out in the spring before planting time, for every member of the family was needed on the farm.

The children sat on long wooden benches. They wrote on slates. The academy was equipped with a pot-bellied stove and a few books. Water was drunk from a gourd dipper from the nearby well. Children attended school in those days as long as they had the urge to do so, or as long as the parents could afford to pay tuition. The few students who could afford to attend high school went to a larger town and boarded with families living in the community.

In 1886, a Christian Church was built in Temple. The school was then held in the new church because it was a larger building and had better accommodations than the small academy.

In 1888, on the site of the present Baptist church, a combination school and lodge hall was constructed. This was a two-story, frame structure. The school held classes on the ground floor and the local Masons and Odd Fellows met on the second. Trustees of the school at the time of construction were J. P. Griffin, J. Q. Riggs, P. I. Sewell, J. T. Copeland, and Z. T. Adams. The officers of Temple Lodge 322 were J. W. Allgood, J. F. Brooks, and I. J. Mathews. The lodges and trustees of the school owned the building. This structure was the third building in which school was held in Temple. It provided much larger quarters than did the first academy or the Christian church. Among the first teachers were Miss Itty Cobb, W. A. Abercrombie, J. R. Spence, Mrs. E. L. Connell, and John Sims.

There were no commencements held at the close of school. Instead, the closing was marked by exhibitions. All of the children participated in this well-attended social event. There were recitations, music, and speeches made by local orators. The exhibitions were the highlight of the school year and were enjoyed by all. At this time in the history of Temple, the school was the center of the social activity.

Some of the early merchants of Temple not already mentioned who did a thriving business included J.E. Levans and J.K. Griffin, Barge and Sewell, Dr. Hamlin C. Cook and John M. Allen Drug Store, E.L. Connell seed business, Baxter Brothers, and J.T. Davis gin.

During the 1890s and early 1900s, the area's successful cotton farming still set the tempo for the business life of Temple. Many rock stores were built. The Temple Banking Company opened in 1903 and by 1912 the Farmers' State Bank was also serving the town.

By 1890, Temple had a population of approximately 250. The firm of Barge and Sewell had just constructed a new store twenty by eighty feet with concrete walls and brick front. Finally, all the merchants replaced their wooden-frame store houses with those of rock, concrete, and brick. In 1890, the town was making plans to light its principal streets. Dave Baxter finished his new store in 1891.

Nearly every family had a flock of chickens, vegetable garden, and fruit trees. Everyone owned a cow or two which provided all the sweet milk, buttermilk, and butter the family could use. They sold chickens, eggs, butter and other farm products to the local merchants. The merchants had chicken coops behind their stores where chickens were kept until they could be sent to the market in Atlanta. Some were sold to local families.

A depression in 1893 was felt by the cotton farmers when the price of cotton fell to nine cents per pound. Corn was selling for 75 cents per bushel and meal was bringing 80 cents per bushel. The year of 1893 was not only a year of low prices, but also a year of short crops. But as farmers always do, they just worked a little harder and did without until things got better. This was their way of life, and making do with what one had was expected.

The following year, 1894, the Georgia Pacific which first breathed life into this place yielded to the wrath of the depression and sold out to the Southern Railway Company. The Norfolk Southern owns the road today.

John and Lula Walker built a large, frame two-story hotel in 1895 on West Sage Street between Montgomery Street and what is now named Old Bremen Road. The hotel was directly across the street from the depot. It was known for its fine food.

Walker's Hotel had eighteen large rooms and a lobby. There was a separate building on the west side which housed the sample room where drummers displayed their wares for the merchants to see.

The hotel was quite something for this small town. It was the scene of much activity as the drummers arrived and departed. The drummers arrived by train and were met at the depot by porters from the hotel. Sometimes there was not enough room and some guests went next door to the home of W.B. Manley to sleep.

The drummers spent several days calling on merchants in and around Temple by hired conveyances. These wagons and buggies were rented from the livery stable. It, like the hotel, did a booming business.

The hotel was bought by Pete and Jane Lewis in 1910. They, too, did a thriving business. The hotel became known as Lewis's Hotel.

Temple became a boom town again. It was a thriving cotton market for a large area. In the fall there were so many bales of cotton in town that they overflowed the warehouses and were piled along the streets and in the churchyards. In order to get to the church doors on Sundays, the people had to walk through narrow paths between the cotton bales.

The four gins were kept running for long hours during the fall. The cotton buyers were kept busy classing and buying the cotton from the farmers. Wagons loaded with cotton formed long lines waiting their turn at the gins.

The cotton oil mill and the depot operated twenty-four hours a day. This was the only way the large amount of cotton could be bought and shipped to market. The livery stable owned by Williams and McColister had to enlarge to take care of their large trade. It was always open. Drummers rented horses and buggies so that they could call on the merchants in the vicinity. Flat wagons called drays were used for delivery purposes.

A favorite pastime for the people was meeting the passenger trains at the depot to see who was leaving or arriving in town. If the train brought mail everyone would then gather at the post office until the mail was put up.

Hundreds of wagons were sold each year in Temple. The Kinney and Steadham store (located on West Johnson St [Hwy 113] near Rome St) would buy them by the carload. Many were sold straight from the freight cars. At times, new wagons for sale were lined up along West Johnson Street extending westward to a point near the end of Sage Street.

From its inception, Temple was a fine business point. It was surrounded by productive farms. Temple was once vividly described as

"a little town which lies on the happiest lines of latitude and longitude
   that girdles Carroll County up in the northern corner where God pours

out His floods of sunshine and showers, where the cotton fields wave
their white banner of peace, and the air comes filtered through jungles
of honeysuckles and roses, under the soft Southern skies where the
mocking bird sings his sweetest song and every heart is as warm as the
noonday sun."

Except for a few minor business slumps, Temple enjoyed prosperous days from 1882 to the late twenties. In 1927 the population was 600. There were two brick churches, two frame churches, one brick school building, three furniture factories, two gins, two grist mills, one cotton seed oil mill, five warehouses, seven filling stations, three shops, two garages, fifteen stores, one bank, one drug store, one millinery store, one dress making shop, one hotel, three restaurants, one dental parlor, one lumber plant, and a city hall. The people were noted for their hospitality and loyalty to the town. The townsmen expressed a need for more factories that would make the payroll of Temple like other towns.

Sage Street clothing merchant Joseph L. Saul was on a business trip to New York to purchase the latest fashions for his store when he received an urgent telegram from an employee. The employee implored Saul to come home at once because a bug was devastating the all important cotton crop and trouble was brewing. Finally, it happened. The feared, dreaded, and loathed boll weevil invaded the fine, profitable cotton fields of Temple.

The Farmers State Bank, located a few doors down from his store, was forced to close and consequently Saul lost money as did many other citizens. The Temple Banking Company closed also. The local economy could no longer support his and other businesses in town. This tragic turn of events was followed by the Great Depression of the 1930s which plunged the town toward economic ruin.

Additionally, the nation's over-production of cotton, and the appearance of synthetic fibers in the textile markets made growing cotton less profitable still. As the cotton market began to wane, bustling and prosperous Temple started to wither and almost died.

Several merchants weathered the depression, however, and remained in business for many years. Claude Morris opened a general merchandise store and later a restaurant in Saul's location which stayed in business until Morris retired and sold to another restaurateur in the 1960s. Dr. C. R. Hart opened a drug store in the Temple Banking Company building which he operated until his retirement in the 1960s. They sold to the farmers who were still growing cotton and corn. Their customers also included those who had chosen to leave the uncertainty of farm life and work for local manufacturing companies and business establishments of Temple and nearby cities.

Temple, with its slower pace, has been a wholesome town in which to live and educate children. The people have remained neighborly and readily come to one's aid during a time of need.

Gone are the depot, hotel, ginneries, blacksmith shops, oil mill, livery stable, and one-room school. The railroad still remains, but most of its ties with this place have faded away. The railroad doesn't transport cotton from here; there is none. Neither does it bring drummers and visitors to town since everyone owns a car. The single passenger train through town doesn't stop. The freight trains that seem endless in length stream through town carrying goods to distant places.

The earth which once was carpeted with lush fields of cotton, corn, wheat, and oats is now canopied with pine trees. Some of the pines were planted several years ago for the pulpwood market, but most were planted by nature as the native, majestic pines released their seeds to the winds. Cattle now graze where once the cotton and corn grew.

The kudzu vine still grows along the roadsides. It is a persistent reminder of the days when farmers used this plant to help control soil erosion and for livestock feed. This fast-growing plant was also used as an ornamental vine. It was planted near the houses to provide shade for the porches. When farm houses were abandoned, the kudzu became rampant and soon covered the decaying farm buildings and trees which once shaded the broom-swept yards.

A few wells with their windlasses, ropes, and well buckets are still used today. These stand as reminders of the day when wells were the main source of water. The cool, refreshing water was drunk from dippers fashioned from long-handled gourds. In later years store bought dippers were also used.

The drawing of a fresh bucket of water and offering a dipper to a visitor was a way of showing hospitality. Complimenting a farmer on his good well water was "music to his ears." A well and gourd dipper were still in use at Caldwell's store in the Abilene community until it too closed awhile back.

A few old barns which have been bleached by the sun to a silvery gray still stand, but not so proudly as they did in days gone by. The wood-shingled roofs, which long ago were covered with tin, have darkened and been turned by rust to a dark red hue.

Even though there are a reminders still present of the days gone by, much of it lingers only as memories in the minds and hearts of men.

CHAPTER VIII

FIRST CHARTER

The first charter of Temple as it appears in *Acts and Resolution of the General Assembly of the State of Georgia*, 1882-1883 is as follows:

Section I. Be it enacted by the General Assembly of the State of Georgia, that from and after the passage of this Act, the town of Temple, in the county of Carroll, be, and the same is hereby incorporated under the name and style of Temple.

Section II. Be it further enacted etc., That the corporate limits of said town shall extend one-half mile wide on each side of the Georgia Pacific Railway, and one-half mile east and one-half mile west of the depot in said town, running parallel with said railway, making the corporate limits one mile wide, running parallel with said railway, and one mile long.

Section III. Be it further enacted by the authority aforesaid, That the provisions in section 774 to section 797 inclusive of the Revised Code of the State of Georgia, 1882, are hereby conferred and granted to the town of Temple, and all the powers, privileges and authorities therein given are hereby made applicable to said town of Temple.

Section IV. Be it further enacted etc., That the first election in said town shall be held on the first Saturday in October, 1883.

Section V. Be it further enacted etc., That no malt, spirituous, or other intoxicating liquors shall be sold within the corporate limits of said town after the passage of this Act, and any person who may violate this section of this Act shall be guilty of a misdemeanor, and on conviction thereof shall be punished as prescribed in section 4310 of the Code of Georgia of 1882.

Section VI. Be it further enacted, etc., That all laws and parts of laws in conflict with this Act be, and the same are hereby repealed.

Approved August 28, 1883.

CHAPTER IX

THE TEMPLE ENTERPRISE

When a *History of Temple, Georgia*, was published in 1982, there were no known copies of Temple's only newspaper, *The Temple Enterprise*, still in existence. Fortunately, a copy has since been found. Thanks to Gary and Sara Parrish a copy of the April 11, 1913 edition of the paper was located in Florida. It belonged to Grace (Mrs. Cliff) Yearty, Sara's aunt. Photocopies of the pages were made. According to a personal account, the newspaper was printed in the two-story building located at the corner of Sage and James Streets. It is hoped the photocopies of this edition and the other research materials, documents, and artifacts used to complete this book will find a permanent home if Temple is able to one day construct a library.

The excerpt below is reproduced from *The Temple Enterprise* dated April 11, 1913 as a small sample from the newspaper:

Article:
Paul Cobb's Horse Runs Away

Last Friday, Paul Cobb, who carries the mail on route 3, had the misfortune to have his horse run away with him, tearing his buggy to splinters. He had to borrow a buggy to finish the mail route. Mr. Cobb was bruised up a little, but not so much he cannot move around.

Personal Notes for Temple

Try Blue Seal Ice Cream at White's Soda Fountain.

G.A. Sharp is courting this week in Carrollton.

J.R. White is at Carrollton this week courting.

Ollie Williams says farming is agreeing with his anatomy.

W.L. Kinney is in Carrollton this week attending court.

Ice Cream any time at Temple Drug Company. We are the best.

Mr. T.F. Woodruff and Lewis Connell, two of Temple's leading salesmen of Dr. Alexander's Healing Oil, were in Villa Rica this Tuesday.

Jesse Kelly had the misfortune of slipping on a banana peeling in Bremen Monday night falling from 36 fracturing his left arm. {note: The number 36 refers to a train locomotive. Mr. Kelly worked for the railroad and is pictured in front of a locomotive in this book.}

The celebrated line of O'Bryan Bros. "Duckhead" Overalls can be found at Kirk and Lewis.

Have you seen our complete line of toilet articles?
Temple Drug Company

We sell three 15 cent cakes of soap for 21 cents.
Temple Drug Company

We use only the purest fruits and extracts at our soda fountain. We sell QUALITY.
Temple Drug Company

We have in bulk fresh Kentucky Wonder and Valentine Seed Beans. Also Watermelon and Cantaloupe Seeds.
Temple Drug Company

Personal Notes for Hickory Level

Tom Willis' barn caught fire last week. No serious damage was done. It caught on fire from the woods.

H.E. Reeves of Villa Rica, has been in this section this past week selling organs.

Lovett Newells, of Carrollton, passed through here Sunday in an auto.

Ask the boys of Hickory Level about their "fishing association" if you would like to join.

Insights into the business life of the community can be gleaned from the advertisements placed in this newspaper: Both the Farmers State Bank and the Temple Banking Company placed advertisements in this particular edition. In an effort to demonstrate solvency in this era before Federal deposit insurance, the Temple Banking Company incorporated their balance sheet in their advertisement. Assets totaled approximately $105,000 whereas an accounting entry for Overdrafts Unsecured totaled less than $5000. The Temple Cotton Oil Company advertised several varieties of fertilizer for sale. A competitor, R. M. Thomason, also advertised a number of fertilizer varieties including Guano, XXX Cotton Grower, and Dissolved Fish Bone. The Williams Barber Shop touted Sharp Razors and Scissors. The Star Pressing Club advertised services in cleaning, pressing, and altering with a specialty in ladies work. One local resident advertised a Milch Cow for sale. {note: pronounced *milch* (just as it is spelled); an Old English word of Germanic extraction for milk.}

CHAPTER X

SCHOOLS

Courtesy, Mrs. Gordon Cole

Temple Academy. Teachers W. A. Abercrombie and John Sims, Circa 1903

At the turn of the century two teachers were teaching more than one hundred children at **TEMPLE ACADEMY**. Teaching methods were very traditional and very much what they had been for years.

The academy was filled to capacity, and the building was not suitable for expansion. A few years before, a windstorm had done considerable damage to the structure. To lessen the chance of the building toppling over, long pine poles had been placed against the north side.

The children sat at homemade desks which were beginning to yield to the years of wear and tear by the energetic scholars. Innumerable initials had been engraved on the desk tops, revealing the identity of once-bored scholars and the childhood romances which were not at all uncommon.

The school in the old, wooden building stood at a turning point. Its destiny lay in the hands of a man whose thinking in the field of education was years ahead of the times. The man who wanted to change all of this was a Carroll County teacher, Ira W. Williams, who held an A.B. Degree from the University of Georgia. He had a dream of expanding the educational opportunities of the farm children far beyond the areas of reading, writing, and arithmetic. Williams had previously taught at Sand Hill and developed some of his ideas there. His home was on a farm south of Villa Rica.

There were two main obstacles in the way of improving the school in Temple. One was the task of convincing the school patrons that completely breaking away from tradition and custom would bring about a better education for the children. The second, and just as difficult if not more so, was the job of raising the large amount of money necessary to build and operate the new school. These two hurdles seemed insurmountable to most people, but Professor Williams dared to try.

He wanted to include the children of farm families in the surrounding communities in his educational program. This involved consolidation and a transportation system; both of which were almost unheard of at the time. "Surely," the people thought, "this man has taken leave of his senses!"

His proposed program included a sound, varied curriculum taught by teachers who were trained, qualified, and willing to move to a small, Southern town.

The children were to be trained to use their hands as well as their minds. This training was to be closely related to farming, the children's way of life. A college preparatory course would also be offered.

Professor Williams diligently worked toward making his dream become a reality. He contacted both local people and prominent men throughout the state and in other states as well. He sold them on the idea and convinced them of the great need. Slowly, many of those contacted began to open up their pocketbooks and give to this cause. Among those who helped financially were the Honorable Hoke Smith and Clark Howell, Editor of the Atlanta Constitution. The new school in its formative stages was given much publicity.

It was proposed that a $5,000 bond issue be voted for the purpose of building the new schoolhouse. There was much local support, but there was also disapproval as was brought out when the bond referendum failed more than once. Many people felt that taxes would increase too much and that the town would never be able to pay off the debt. Finally, in 1903 the bonds were approved by the voters.

A View of the School Building and Conveyances.

Courtesy, Paul Cobb

A View of the Temple Model School and Conveyances, Circa 1904

Temple Model School Wagons, 1904

The new school was to be a model school, "**TEMPLE MODEL SCHOOL**," whose graduates would be prepared for farming, to enter college, and teach in the smaller, rural schools.

Hamp Sewell was the mayor of the town at the time. The town councilmen were M.E. Griffin, J.S. Dobbs, W.M. Cobb, G.W. Roop, and M.T. Marchman. The building committee was composed of E.L. Connell, E.H. Gober, G.S. Mathews, and W.A. Enterkin.

In the summer of 1903, the contract for construction of the new school was let. The structure was to be a two-story, brick building consisting of four classrooms on the ground floor and an auditorium on the second. The roof was to be covered with shingles of slate. The site chosen for the school was the corner of James and Griffin Streets; the building was to face the business district of town. A belfry to house a giant bell, which would summon the youngsters to class, was included in the plans.

Early in 1904, the new, brick building was completed. It stood majestically overlooking the town. The bell pealed clearly, announcing that the dream of a brave man had come true. An attempt to provide better education for rural children was finally coming to life by way of leadership from a man who dared to have faith, confidence, and courage.

The completion of the new building and the anticipation of better schooling was a time of rejoicing in the small town of Temple. The new schoolhouse stood proudly awaiting the sound of the bell which would call the children to class and bring life and spirit to the quiet rooms and halls.

33

The Board of Directors of the new school were E.L. Connell, President; J.A. Griffin; W.P. Muse; T.M. Spruell; and C.L. Baskin.

At the opening of the school, the faculty was composed of Ira W. Williams, Superintendent; J. Philander Campbell, Sr., Assistant Superintendent; Mrs. Laura Josephine Rozar, Wesleyan College, Principal High School; Miss Jessye Swope, State Normal School, Principal Model School; Miss Isabelle S. Thursby, Oread, Maryland, Domestic Science and Manual Training High School; Miss Evelyn Dimon, State Normal School, Fourth and Fifth Grades; Miss Ella Griffin, LaGrange Female College, Second and Third Grades; Miss Vannie Hunt, State Normal School, First Grade; and Madam Dell Antonio, Vienna, Austria, Music.

The cornerstone exercises were under the auspices of Temple Masonic Lodge, No. 322 F. & A. M. This occasion was attended by many local people on hand to share the excitement of the day. Coins and other mementos were placed behind the stone in a copper box. The second brick schoolhouse in the county was now complete.

Loyal Cobb, a former student of the school, had a handbook produced by the Model School in 1904. The very informative booklet covered all aspects of the program of the school along with representative pictures. The purpose of the school was also recorded:

"It is the purpose of the school to give the people of the rural districts that
training which prepares them for life, in addition to a good literary education.
Consolidation, transportation, and industrial work enable us to do this, and it
is our purpose to develop them to the highest degree of perfection."

The transportation system was the first in the state. The buses were mule and horse-drawn wagons with covered tops and side curtains which were lowered in bad weather. Some of the wagons were equipped with small, coke heaters. The wagons would seat about twenty children on long benches built on each side. The driver of each wagon lived at the furthermost point along the route and stopped to pick up students along the way. There were two drivers for each wagon. The drivers either attended school or worked on the rented, school farm to produce feed for the animals. One of the early drivers was Otis Camp who drove two beautiful, black horses called George and Dan by the scholars. Other drivers included Paul Astin, J. Phil Campbell, Sr., Henry Holcombe, Andrew Deese, Marvin Evans, Millard Nesselhunt, Charles Wynne, and Joe Biggers. Children were transported from Draketown, Center Point, Station 48, Hickory Level, District Line, Wesley Chapel, Mount Carmel, Brooklyn, and other surrounding communities. Other students boarded with local families for eight to ten dollars a month. Some students came to school by private conveyances.

Parents of children living in Temple supported the school financially on a planned basis. Non-resident pupils were charged $1.25 to $3.00 per month tuition. The older students paid the larger amount.

John F. Brooks, who later became Carroll County School Superintendent, led in the development in the new and unique transportation system. With Mr. Williams leadership and that of Phil Campbell, Sr., the school was expanded to ten grades. Casper Lassetter of near Villa Rica was the school's first graduate having attended one year.

Two courses of study were offered. A college preparatory program included English, Latin, Greek, botany, geology, physics, chemistry, physiology, algebra, geometry, trigonometry, history, geography, drawing, manual training, agriculture, farm engineering, surveying, and political economy. A college preparatory student could complete the fourth year of Latin and two of Greek by the end of the tenth grade. The terminal student, after completion of the seventh grade, took such courses as agriculture, farm engineering, drawing, and manual training for boys. The course for girls included sewing, painting, and domestic science. The primary graded school offered reading, writing, arithmetic, and geography. They also were involved in nature study, clay modeling, and paper cutting. American history, Georgia history, and government were included in the courses for the upper elementary grades.

All grades were involved in suitable manual training courses which were closely related to farming activities. The school rented a farm at which the principles learned in class were put into practice. Farming activities were mainly planned for the older boys. The younger students became involved in vegetable garden work. Local merchants supported the school by furnishing guano and farm supplies.

The Georgia High School Association had its beginning in Temple in 1905. At that time, Dr. Joseph Stewart was at the University of Georgia mainly to work with the high schools in the state. While performing his duties as high school inspector and high school representative, he and Laura J. Rozar organized the Northwest Georgia High School Association. In 1906, the group met at Buchanan. During the day the principals, teachers, and school officers met to discuss the development of a course of study for the high schools, means of support, and other topics dealing with the operation of the high schools. In the afternoon there were athletic contests among the schools and at night an elocution contest was held.

The Temple Model School became one of the first schools to teach agriculture classes in high school. Agricultural and homemaking education which was begun at Temple in 1904 received statewide endorsement in 1906 when the law was passed establishing eleven congressional district agricultural and mechanical schools in the state.

The Temple Model School lasted only for a brief and shining period. Though soliciting and receiving sizable gifts from people in Atlanta and elsewhere, the school made financial commitments that it was unable to meet. The community not only lacked the financial resources to maintain such a school, but the community's conservative outlook often clashed with the progressive ideas of Ira W. Williams and his staff.

At the close of the 1907 term, the school resumed a more conventional program, but it remained one of the best village schools in the county. Though many of the students returned to their rural schools, many remained and boarded in private homes while completing their high school educations.

All was not lost when the school changed directions. School superintendent Ira W. Williams continued many of the innovations developed at Temple Model School when he became a consultant to the 4th district A&M School, a forerunner of The University of West Georgia. The "seeds" that were sown at Temple Model School had influence on education in Georgia for many years.

TEMPLE GRADED SCHOOL. In the school year 1908-1909, Temple issued a booklet entitled "Announcement for the Temple Graded School." The booklet consisted of a picture of the school and information dealing with all phases of the school's activities. The principal was W.A. Shelton who had an A.B. degree from the University of Georgia. Miss Lillie Culbertson, a graduate of the Georgia Normal and Industrial School, taught the first and second grades. The third and fourth grade teacher was Miss Ella Griffin, who had special preparation for grade work at the Summer School of the South and Columbia University. Miss Eloise Connell, who also graduated from Georgia Normal, taught the fifth and sixth grades. Miss Kate Woodruff, instructor in vocal and instrumental music, completed the staff. The Board of Education for the year included Dr. Charles L. Baskin, President; W.W. Edmondson, Secretary; W.P. Muse, Treasurer; W.L. Kinney and J.A. Griffin.

The first page of "Announcement for Temple Graded School" was entitled "The New System" and stated:

"In compliance with an act of the Legislature of 1907 establishing a public school in the town of Temple, Georgia, following the election held September 7, 1907, the Temple Graded School will be opened August 24, 1908, for the first term under the school tax system.

The increase in funds enable the Board of Education to employ more teachers, to offer free tuition within the town limits, and to reduce the rates to non-resident pupils. The Temple Graded School is now on a firm financial basis and its efficiency will increase. Parents who would educate their children should not, and will not, hesitate long to locate in Temple."

The tuition for non-resident students was reduced; the elementary grades by $0.25 per month and high school by $0.50. An incidental fee of $0.75 was charged all pupils at the beginning of the year.

The handbook included a thorough set of rules for the Board of Education, along with the order of the proceedings. The Board's expectations of the principal, teachers, pupils, and patrons were given. The expectations were high.

A course of study complete with title and authors of textbooks was listed for all grades. High school students could pursue either a literary or business course of study. Eudell Scott had a copy of the handbook.

In 1914, the school was known as **TEMPLE PUBLIC SCHOOL.** The school was quite traditional and the teachers stressed the three "R's." The teachers were well qualified and did not mind using the hickory stick on occasion.

The informational booklet printed by the school for the 1914-1915 school year is quite complete and reflects the strengths and structure of the school program. The school was a vital part of the town during this time and received strong support from its patrons. Sara Hamrick had a copy of this booklet.

The school staff for 1914-1915 was composed of J.B. Parham, Principal; Miss Mae Laird; Miss Ruth Levans; Miss Clara Carswell; and Miss Carrie Davidson. Mrs. Hattie Steed was the principal of the school for African-American students with Mike Sumerlin serving as her assistant.

In 1920, bonds had been passed and an annex was built behind the school. The single-story, brick structure contained four classrooms and a library.

The eleventh grade was added to Temple High School in 1925. The first graduates to complete eleven grades were Tommy Raburn, Lois Smith, Clara Bell Kinney, Agnes Kinney, Hazel White, Morine Allgood, Hugh Adams, John Taylor, and John Thomas Steadham.

In 1929, the Center Point School consolidated with Temple. Cecil Spence transported the children to school over all the dirt roads.

Oftentimes, the county did not have enough money to pay the salaries of the teachers. When this was the case the board issued certificates of indebtedness (scrip) to the teachers in the amount due them. The scrip was paid off by the county as the money became available. Sometimes teachers would turn the scrip over to a bank or business man and receive a reduced amount. This person later collected from the school board.

Each school had its own local board of education known as the Local Board of Trustees. The trustees were elected by the registered voters on the last Saturday in July of the coming school year. The member designated as the secretary-treasurer looked after all the money matters and received a small monthly salary for his/her services. Some years later the trustees were appointed by the Grand Jury. The local boards were discontinued in 1973.

In the school year 1931-1932, the teachers were Miss Hazel Smith, Mrs. J.R. Baxter, Miss Lil Connell, Miss Annice Lipford, Mrs. Cranston Hamil and Carlos Hamil. Cranston Hamil was the principal.

The words to the Alma Mater were written in 1933 by Miss Mary Hays, a Temple High School English teacher. The beautiful song is still sung at Temple High.

On September 4, 1934, residents of the Brooklyn community went before the County Board and requested to consolidate with Temple. E.C. Karr drove the bus from Brooklyn. His bus had a wooden body that he built himself. Instead of glass in the windows there were heavy curtains which were lowered to keep out the rain and cold.

During the 1934-1935 school year, the principal of Temple School made $1,350. The teachers' salaries varied from $540 to $720 for the year. During this year, L.D. Spear was the principal of the African-American school, and Claudia Spear was a teacher there.

Finances were so uncertain in 1936-1937 that the County Board reserved the right to make changes in teachers' salaries at any time or meeting.

Discontinued schools in the area not already noted included Bold Springs, Bethel, Taylors, Brooks, Mt. Carmel, Lovells, Pine Grove, and Hickory Level.

A hot lunch program was initiated in the fall of 1937 with the P.T.A. as sponsor. The lunches were prepared and served in the canning plant at the price of 5 cents. Milk and plenty of vegetables were served by the volunteer mothers. Mrs. Cecil Levans was the manager and only paid employee. Her salary was $12.50 per week. Henry Cartwright, local merchant, supplied the lunchroom with commodities at wholesale prices. The program received a few dollars of federal funds.

Temple School, 1939-1985

In mid-August of 1939, a brick-veneered building was opened on east Sage Street. Approximately 300 students were enrolled in grades one through eleven. Due to insufficient space, the first grade remained in the old building for several years.

Many tall chimneys reached skyward from the roof of the new school since the rooms were heated with coal burning, pot-bellied heaters. The heaters were enclosed with huge, metal "jackets" designed to make them more serviceable. On several occasions, a mischievous boy could overload a heater with coal, making the back of the room extremely hot and uncomfortable. Needless to say, the class was interrupted while windows and doors were flung open for cool air.

The structure was H-shaped with the high school occupying the front wing and six elementary rooms in the back. The two sections were joined by an auditorium.

The high school wing consisted of five classrooms, science laboratory, library, principal's office, kitchen and a book storage room. Since there was no dining area, the pupils and teachers picked up their lunches in the kitchen and carried them to their desks. The kitchen was later moved to a larger room. Homemade tables with benches attached were then used on one side of the kitchen and in part of the hallway.

At this time, the school remained the center of the community activities. The auditorium was always filled to capacity when plays, operettas, graduations, country music shows, and other functions were presented.

The building was constructed under the Public Works Administration which was part of President Franklin Roosevelt's New Deal. Wm. J.J. Chase of Atlanta was the architect and the Newman Construction Company of LaGrange was the contractor. The Temple School Trustees at the time of construction were C.E. Stallings, Chairman; C.R. Hart, Secretary-Treasurer; C.H. Wester; H.L. Cartwright; and G.R. Teel. W.O. Smith was the principal. Dr. Guy Wells, a native of Temple and then president of Georgia State College for Women, planned, financed, and supervised the landscaping of the school grounds.

At this time, there were three bus drivers, E.C. Karr, Cecil Spence, and Olin Johnson.

All students attended chapel in the auditorium each week. The pupils were required to enter and leave the auditorium in single file and with mouths closed. Each grade had assigned rows on which to sit. The senior class was given special privileges. Among these was the honor of sitting at the front of the auditorium. They were the first to enter and leave the auditorium – always accompanied by the pianist with a march.

A custom practiced for many years by the seniors took place on April Fools' Day. The class left the campus without permission, walked around the loop, and returned to school. The principal had a forgiving spirit on that day and usually ignored the happening.

Although the heyday for farming was over, many children still lived on farms where cotton was grown. In order for the students to pick cotton in the fall, a six-week summer session was held. School was then turned out for six weeks in the fall for crop harvesting.

A trip to Washington, D.C. was taken by the senior class each spring. The arrival of class rings and the trip were the highlights for this class. The trip was financed by various fund-raising projects such as the presentation of an annual play and selling snacks at recess time. For years the trip was made by school bus with a local driver. Later, the trip was made by either commercial buses or train. These trips were suspended during World War II. After the war, the trips were resumed and extended to include New York. After a few years, the annual class trip was discontinued.

Basketball games and all activities requiring the use of school buses were discontinued during the war. The buses were only used to transport children to and from school. This was because gasoline was rationed and could not be used for non-essential travel. The school did not have a basketball coach during the war years. There were no athletic activities.

There was a teacher shortage during the war since many of them were either in military service or working in defense plants. It was not uncommon for a class to have several teachers in one year with some of them staying for only one or two months. Oftentimes the temporary teachers were retirement age who had been called back into service to keep the schools open.

In 1948, the community, under the leadership of D.F. Staples, principal, bought an army building at Fort Oglethorpe, Georgia. High school boys and men of the community dismantled the building, hauled it to Temple, and reconstructed it directly behind the school as a gymnasium. Though crude by the standards of today, it served the school well as its first gym. A small blackboard served as a scoreboard. Bill Thomas was the coach. Roy Baxter was the chairman of the building committee.

The twelfth grade was added in the 1951-1952 school year. The first to graduate from the twelfth grade were Bonnell Roberson, Mac Hamil, Katherine Redding, Bobby Ingram, Sue Ivey, Bill Green, Mary Anderson, and Kenneth Holt.

During the 1951-1952 school year, the high school printed a newspaper, "The Eagle's Eye." Jane Hixon was the first editor, and Mrs. Julia Carroll was the faculty sponsor. The paper eventually fell by the wayside in later years. In 1968, the idea was revived and "Tiger Prints" came into existence. Miss Kathy Thomas was faculty sponsor. Pam Pointer, a fourth-grade student, entered the contest for naming the newspaper and submitted the name which was selected.

The first Temple School yearbook, *Memories,* was printed in 1952 by the Senior Class. Mrs. J.R. Livingston served as faculty sponsor, and Bonnell Roberson was the first editor. The annual retained this name until 1956 when it was changed to *Tiger.* The tiger is also the school mascot. School colors are gold and black.

Two, wood-frame classrooms were attached to the east side of the gym in 1955. They were first used as elementary classrooms. Later, the partition between the rooms was removed and the area was converted into a home economics department which had previously been in the main building.

In 1957, a new lunchroom was constructed southeast of the elementary wing. It was a cement block and jumbo brick structure. A three-room elementary school addition was built to the east of the main building at the same time.

Improvements to the school structure were planned for the summer of 1957. The Carroll County Board of Education contracted with a firm to modernize the lighting and plumbing. Central heat was to replace the old pot-bellied heaters.

As a preliminary measure, the contractors "burned out" the old, chemical toilets. Evidently they were inexperienced with such a contrivance because the fire got too hot and set the building on fire. The entire elementary section and over one-half the auditorium were destroyed. With the help of the Temple Volunteer Fire Department, fire departments from surrounding towns, and a downpour of rain, the high school was saved from destruction.

At the beginning of school in the fall of 1957, three elementary classes moved into the new classroom structure, one class moved to the Baptist Church and two classes were housed in the Methodist Church.

Plans were immediately made to restore the auditorium and rebuild the elementary classrooms. These rooms were built to the west of the original building on the site of the grandstand and baseball diamond. The facility was completed in 1959. The classes housed in the churches returned to the campus.

A new gymnasium was built west of the new elementary rooms in 1960. There was only enough money to build bleachers on one side of the gym. Parents and friends of the school donated money to build seats on the other side.

The new Providence School was built in 1958 on Otis Street. It replaced a frame, army building which had been serving as the school on the same site. Prior to the army building, the Afican-American students attended classes on the ground floor of the Masonic Lodge on Rome Street.

After completing elementary school at Providence, the students went to Carver High School in Carrollton.

In the fall of 1965, the Carroll County Board of Education implemented a desegregation plan known as "freedom of choice." This meant that students could attend either school. The Carver High School students who chose to attend Temple High during the first year of the plan were Glenda Ware, Melvin Keller, Charles Shanks, Lawrence Beedles, James Beedles, Phillip Gray, Jerome Luke, William Arney, Virginia Arnold, Gwendolyn Helton, and Janice Gray. The first African-American graduate of Temple High was Glenda Ware in 1966.

A total desegregation plan was put into effect in the fall of 1968. All African-American students living in the Temple attendance area transferred to the other school. Providence Elementary became Temple Primary for all the first and second graders. All students in grades three through twelve attended school at the elementary and high school on East Sage.

Federal funds were made available in December 1965 for a kindergarten class at the primary school. These funds were provided through the Elementary and Secondary Education Act.

In November 1974, the voters of the county passed a bond referendum for $5,000,000 for an extensive building program. Included in the program was a new high school in Temple costing $741,500 and completed in the fall of 1976 – Roy Denney and Associates, architects; Richards and Associates, contractors. The site of construction was next to the old high school on lots bought from Earl Morrow and Roy Brazeal.

A new Temple High School was completed in 1976.

The public schools of Temple received a boost in 1976 when a new high school opened for the fall term. The new building resulted from a 1974 county bond referendum in which Temple voters gave their overwhelming support of 72% of the voters voting in favor of the bonds. The sixteen classrooms and related facilities alleviated the over-crowded conditions which had plagued the school for a number of years.

The building committee included Ronald D.Sikes, Sandra Edge, Melissa Smith, Ruth Holder, Charlotte Doyal, Bobby Gentry, Harry Shadrix, Bobby Pope, and Burell Holder.

The first school band was organized in 1973 when Ronald D. Sikes was principal. Susan Lipford Ogletree was the first director. Also, a lobby and dressing rooms were added to the gymnasium.

In the field of sports, Coach Donald Stitcher's basketball team won the State Class B championship in 1978. The State Tournament is sponsored by the Georgia High School Association which had its beginning in Temple in 1905.

The championship team consisted of Lorraine Spidell, Lynn Pope, Donna Conaway, Susan Holloman, Pam Billings, Denise Dobbs, Tammie Drew, Esther Luke, and Diane Luke. A special honor came to Temple Tigerette Donna Conaway when she was named the Atlanta Constitution Player of the Year.

Throughout the years as the school enrollment has increased, the schools have gone through renovations and additions. Temple now has four schools within the city limits. Each school has a principal. The schools are: Temple Elementary, 95 Otis Street, Grades Pre-K-5 with an enrollment of approximately 485; Providence Elementary, which opened in 2010 and was named for a former African-American school, 287 Rainey Road, Grades Pre-K-5, with an enrollment of approximately 379; Temple Middle School, 275 Rainey Road, Grades 6-8, with an enrollment of approximately 470; and Temple High School, 589 Sage Street, Grades 9-12, with an enrollment of approximately 611. There were 131 seniors in the 2011-2012 school year. In 2002-2003, the high school underwent a major renovation and in 2007-2008 a Freshman Academy was completed. A new gym and an addition to the cafeteria will be completed in 2012. Sandra Morris is our District 2 representative on the Carroll County Board of Education.

On May 5, 2006, the Administration Building at Temple High School was named in honor of Dorothy Burton-Callaway, a former teacher at the school and the first African-American to be elected to the Carroll County Board of Education. She served twelve years. The gymnasium at the high school was named in honor of Coach Donald Stitcher on December 17, 1989. The media center was named the Ruth Holder Media Center on June 11, 1993. Football was started in Temple in 1988. The football stadium, which was completed in 1992, was named the Rogers Stadium in honor of Principal Denzil Rogers. Volunteers from the Athletic Booster Club, the Band Booster Club and the Parent-Teacher Organization staffed a concession stand at the Atlanta-Fulton County Stadium to help pay for the Temple stadium.

Beginning in 1904, the principals include Ira W. Williams, Mrs. L.J. Rozar, W.A. Shelton, J.B. Parham, H.F. Hogg, Miss Tassie Reid, T.H. Shackleford, J.M. Cutts, S.M. Hearn, C.H. King, A.L. Bevis, a Mr. Trammell, W.W. Linton, J.F. Lee, F.G. Spearman, Cranston Hamil, H.P. Bell, Carlos Hamil, W.O. Smith, J.W. Shadix, D.W. Harper, Mrs. Homer L. Turner, Miss Harriet Gallagher, Miss Crawford Roberts, O.L. Entrekin, D.F. Staples, J.R. Livingston, Roy Brazeal, Ronald D. Sikes, Leon Frost, Denzil Rogers, Chuck Taylor, Steve James, Bob Heaberlin, Michael Angresano, Chancey Nash and Karen Suddeth.

Over one hundred years have gone by since the first schoolmaster of Temple, E. Lewis Connell, taught youngsters in this little town. The torch of knowledge that he first set afire has been passed from year to year. Each new principal and teacher strives to help mold the lives of the scholars so that they may find a meaningful place in the world.

CHAPTER XI

THE MEDICAL FIELD

The practice of medicine was begun in Temple almost as soon as the rumblings of the first train through town faded away. Doctors James Brooks and Richard L. Rowe were the first doctors. They opened the first drugstore in town which bore the name of Brooks and Rowe.

Dr. DeLone W. Dorsett became the third doctor to practice medicine here. He opened his office in March 1884. Ten more doctors "hung out their shingles" in Temple before the turn of the century. They were: W.W. Carmical and John T. Cobb, 1889; T. Oscar Bryant, 1891; Thompson M. Spruell, 1892; Reuben P. Durrett and Hamlin C. Cook, 1893; Wyot M. Smith, Charles L. Baskin, and J.B. Golden, 1895; and Buna R. Moore, 1899.

This was the era when doctors traveled by pack horse and horse and buggy. This was the time when doctors kept their medical bags packed and ready for calls both day and night. They went to administer to the sick regardless of the weather or how many hours of sleep they had the night before. They went regardless of the conditions of the narrow, dirt roads.

The men of medicine were not always paid for their services because cotton farmers had very little money except when they sold their cotton in the fall. Even then, it took most of it to pay the debts incurred during the year. The doctors went to see the sick even when the family was too poor to pay. Many times doctors were given farm products rather than money. A load of stove wood might be delivered by a farmer and presented to the doctor in payment for the delivery of a baby.

The physicians were highly respected members of the community. The wives of the doctors were also held in high esteem. They, too, were an important part of the medical practice. The wife kept the doctor's bag packed. She gave him encouragement, she ran the home, and cared for the children. When her husband left in the middle of a stormy night, her night of rest was also over. She waited, worried, and prayed until he arrived safely back home.

On his calls the doctor was never too busy to visit awhile with the farm families. Conversations might go from discussing remedies for the baby's colic to the price of cotton, then on to politics or a little bit of spicy local news.

An epidemic of typhoid fever plagued the early residents for several years from 1883. The doctors did the best they could in coping with the disease. Hardly a family escaped it completely. Most cases recovered from the "slow fever"; some did not. Malaria fever was also a threat, as was consumption and contagious childhood diseases.

The whole community was thrown into a panic when there was a report of a mad dog in town. Occasionally someone was bitten. A common treatment was the application of a mad stone to the wound. The stone would adhere to the wound for hours before dropping off. It supposedly drew the poison from the wound.

SPRINGVILLE HYGIENIC HOME

(Commonly known and ignorantly called Cold Water Cure)

IS PERMANENTLY LOCATED NEAR THE GEORGIA PACIFIC RAILROAD, THREE MILES NORTHWEST OF TEMPLE, GA.

THE ABOVE HEALTH INSTITUTE was opened on the first day of March, 1886, for the reception of all sick persons diseased in every way, and especially ladies in all their different conditions.

There is no treatment so sanative as the Hygienic treatment is to ladies during the periods of pregnancy and labor, and especially during labor and after parturition. The treatment will correct all morbid conditions and enable Nature to perform her proper functions during labor. It will prevent puerperal fever and assist a rapid recovery.

The Above Infirmary Possesses all the Modern Improvements that are Necessary to Carry on the Hygienic Treatment in all its Protean Shapes.

No Poisonous Medicines or Noxious Drugs will be used in any form, but everything will be used that bears a nominal relation to the vital organism, as Water of all Temperatures, Air, Light, Temperature, Electricity, Magnetism, Exercise, Rest, Diet, Sleep, Clothing, Mental Influences, and Mechanical or Surgical Appliances.

My knowledge of the Hygienic Theory, and thirty-five years of experience and practice in the sick room—with strict obedience and perseverance on the part of the patient to all the laws of Hygiene and the rules and regulations of the Institute— enables me to make good the assertion that I can cure permanently all curable cases and greatly benefit those incurable.

I claim almost invariable success in the treatment of Obstetrics and all forms of Uterine Diseases and Displacements.

ALL ACUTE AND CHRONIC DISEASES, AS AGUES, CHILLS, FEVERS, AND INFLAMMATIONS OF ALL KINDS, NEURALGIA AND RHEUMATISM.

All varieties of Bowel Complaints, Consumption in its earlier stages, Dyspepsia, Asthma, Liver, Kidney and Skin Diseases, Constipation and Piles in their most obstinate forms, Gonorrhœa and Spermatorrhœa.

Diseases of every kind are scientifically treated without drugs in any form, while the Hygienic treatment is mild and pleasant and equally adapted and efficacious to every case and at all seasons of the year.

The clime in which the Health Institute is situated is quiet, private, pleasant and healthy, water good and air pure.

As for an Invalid's Summer and Winter Resort, No Better Can be Found.

Each person remaining at this Hygienic Home for board or treatment will be required to strictly conform to all the rules and regulations.

Patients and boarders are all cordially invited to come. We like to have anyone visit us who is pleasant and agreeable, and especially the sick. It has been my daily occupation two-thirds of my life to wait on them. Anyone visiting us we will endeavor to treat as gentlemen and ladies, and give to them our kindest sympathies and prompt attention.

All bills must be paid in advance or good notes given.

All acute cases will be charged $1.50 per day for treatment, board and room, and may be $2.00 per day, on account of unnecessary and extra trouble and night attention.

All chronic cases will be charged $1.00 per day for treatment, board, bedding and rooms, and may be $1.50 per day, on account of unnecessary and extra trouble and night attention.

Ladies will be charged $7.00 for confinement, a room and two weeks' treatment; they furnish their board, bedding and washing.

Boarders only will be charged $8.00 per month. Will be charged more for less time and access to bath rooms and for extra trouble.

J. M. ARMSTRONG, M.D.,
TEMPLE, GA.

Courtesy, Miss Mae Hill

A very unique hospital was established three miles northwest of town on the Draketown Road on March 1, 1886. The hospital was built in the edge of Haralson County on the bank of a small creek. The Springville Hygienic Home was built by Dr. J.M. Armstrong and was known locally as Armstrong's Hospital. Temple residents called the services of the institute the "water cure."

In Dr. Armstrong's advertisements he stated that he used no poisonous medicines, or noxious drugs, but used everything that bore a nominal relation to the vital organs: water of all temperatures, air, light, temperature, electricity, magnetism, exercise, rest, diet, sleep, clothing, mental influences, and surgical or mechanical appliances.

According to the doctor, diseases of every kind were scientifically treated without drugs in any form. The hygienic treatment was stated to be mild and pleasant and equally adapted and efficacious in every case and at all seasons of the year.

Chronic cases were charged $1.00 per day for treatment, room and board, or $1.50 if they caused extra trouble or required night attention. Acute cases were charged $1.50 per day or $2.00 if they caused extra trouble or required night attention. The hospital also served as a summer and winter resort for invalids. These boarders were charged $8 per month.

Dr. Armstrong claimed that due to his knowledge of the Hygienic Theory, and thirty-five years of experience and practice in the sickroom – with strict obedience and perseverance on the part of the patient to all the laws of hygiene and the rules and regulations of the Institute – enabled him to make good the assertion that he could cure permanently all curable cases and greatly benefit those incurable.

The hospital flourished for awhile, but in 1888 the doctor closed his hospital and moved elsewhere in the state.

Alexander's Healing Oil Ad, 1928

Another unusual phase of the medical world was present in Temple during the early 1900s. This was Dr. W.H. Alexander's Healing Oil which was mixed in a washtub at a local drugstore. As the ingredients were mixed it seemed to boil. Dr. C.L. Baskin and Tom Woodruff were partners in the production of the medicine.

The healing oil received its name from Dr. W.H. Alexander, a veterinarian in Cave Spring, who developed it for use on livestock. It proved so effective that is was offered to local citizens as an external "cure all." Woodruff was a salesman for the product and traveled from store to store in this section of the state. The wonderful healing oil could be found in almost every home.

In 1911, Dr. Claud Griffin, a graduate of Temple Model School, began his practice. He was followed by John R. Turner in 1913 and in 1919 by Hulett H. Askew, who later became a well-known surgeon.

Courtesy, Roy Spruell

Dr. T.M. Spruell
Practiced in Temple 1892-1947

Some of the physicians practiced here for only a few years before moving to other locations. Others spent their entire medical careers here. Dr. Spruell was a beloved doctor here who gave untiringly for over fifty-five years from 1892 until his retirement in 1947.

After Dr. Spruell's retirement, there was no doctor serving in Temple until 1958 when Dr. John L. Dorough retired as Director of the Mississippi Health Dept. and moved to Temple. He bought a house on West Sage Street and practiced on a limited basis. He was allegedly a millionaire having gained most of his wealth through long years in the stock market. To a much lesser degree, he accumulated wealth by "keeping everything and discarding nothing." An example of his thriftiness was shown when he broke tongue depressors into two pieces and used only one part when examining a patient's throat. Dr. Dorough often related the fact that he learned to be "saving" during the depression of the 1930s and, thereafter, never departed from his habit. After his death in 1970 Temple was again without a resident doctor.

The Carroll County Health Department opened a clinic at Temple Baptist Church in 1952 under the sponsorship of the P.T.A. It was later moved to a room at the Stephens-Stovall service station at the corner of east Sage Street and Hwy 78. It was then moved to the city hall. The clinic was open one day each week by county health nurse Miss Bessie Rowe and assisted by volunteer Mrs. Frank Lambert and others.

Drugstores in Temple were operated under many names: Brooks and Rowe; G.T. Williams and Dr. Dorsett; Temple Drug Co., owned by Dr. Spruell and Dr. Orr; S.B.J. Drug Co.; Dr. Hamlin C. Cook and John M. Allen; Dr. Buna Moore; J.R. White; Martin and James Marchman; Davis Pharmacy, owned by Lewis T. Davis; John Connell; Hart Drug Co., owned by Dr. C.R. Hart; and Temple Pharmacy, owned by Max Conner and later Jim McWilliams. Dr. Hart operated a drugstore here for almost forty years (1925-1964).

Among the midwives in Temple were Kansas Scales and her daughter, Odie Bell Robinson.

In March 1975, the Temple Medical Clinic opened in the building on West Sage Street formerly occupied by the city hall. Dr. Nasser Tahmassebi of Washington, D.C. practiced here for a short time until the arrival of Dr. Behram Makulu who practiced here over two decades.

In 1998, Tanner Medical System opened a health care facility at 253 Hwy 78. The Rapha Clinic of West Georgia occupies this building now. It is a nonprofit clinic which provides a comprehensive range of services for individuals without the means to afford needed health care. Sue Brockman is the executive director.

Temple Medical Clinic, located at 431 Sage Street, is staffed by Lori Hudson, a nurse practitioner. Dr. Allen Culpepper's office is located at 40 Villa Rosa Road. Manna Medical and Counseling Services is located at 305 Carrollton Street behind Fred's. Karen Powell owns Southern Comfort Personal Care Home at 580 Old Bremen Road.

CHAPTER XII

POST OFFICES

Temple Mail Wagons

Before 1900, there were approximately eighty-four post offices established in the county. Many of them sprang up where there was a store, grist mill, gin or voting place. These small communities often bore colorful names, although they frequently took the name of their first postmaster. Many of them were discontinued after a short time. The postmasters received their pay on a fee system which usually amounted to only a small amount.

Early post offices near Temple were Buck Horn, Simsville, Horace, Birtha, established January 28, 1897, with June Waddell as first postmaster and discontinued in 1898; Berlene, established February 16, 1898, north of Temple with James K. Haney as first postmaster and discontinued in 1898; Coraxi, established June 23, 1899, north of Temple with John C. Hicks as first postmaster and discontinued in 1900; and Lilac, established April 18, 1900, south of Temple with Elijah M. Yates as first postmaster and discontinued in 1902.

Rural Free Delivery of the early 1900s made the small post offices no longer needed. The rural mail routes were formed by prospective mail carriers mapping a route and then getting the people to sign up for mail delivery. If they got enough subscribers, new routes were started.

The post office in Temple was established April 24, 1882, which was over a year before the town was chartered. It was located on West Sage Street in the building next to the present Temple Pharmacy. James H. Allen was appointed postmaster on this date and served until October 15, 1887. From this date until around 1915, the following held this office: Richard L. Rowe, Miss Myrtie Craven, Van R. Davis, Thomas B. Griffin, and Walker M. Cobb.

On January 22, 1915, Warner A. Enterkin was appointed postmaster. About this time the post office was moved to the 2-story building on Sage Street at James Street. It remained there for approximately ten years before being moved to near the middle of the block next door to the location once occupied by Steadham's clothing store.

From September 1, 1923, the following have held the position of postmaster or postmistress: Thomas E. Kirk, Miss Maude E. Sewell, Miss Morine Allgood (Mrs. Homer McColister), Alvin B. Crews, W.F. Lambert, and Hugh W. Hudsputh, who held a lengthy service from 1952 until retiring in 1983. Those serving since are Johnny Muse, John M. Frossard, and Shanon Brown.

In 1959, the post office was moved into a new building built by Bill Steadham at 24 Carrollton Street next to the Methodist Church.

Rural Free Delivery was established in Temple February 1, 1902. At one time four rural routes served the postal area. Some years later they were combined into two routes. In 1982, the routes served over 3000 patrons with a combined mileage of 187 miles.

Records show that the following have served as rural carriers from the Temple office as of 1982: Jethro A Mobley, David H. Mobley, Howard B. Sims, Eldorado H. Cobb, Minnie T. Cobb, Robert T. Sims, George S. Allgood, Charley E. Stallings, Paul Cobb, Charles W. Griffin, Georgia Griffin, Dude Enterkin, J.W. Askew, a Mr. Hollifield, W.O. Lewis, W.F. Lambert, J.W. Hixon, J.F. Lambert, K.H. Elliott, David Osborne, and Mark Haney.

Sage Street Storefront Post Office, 1925-1959
Hugh Hudsputh, Postmaster, and Donald Levans

Temple Post Office on Carrollton Street, 1959-91

Courtesy, Carroll Publishing Company

Rick Palmer, Postal Service Coordinator, presented Postmaster Hugh Hudsputh a commemorative certificate at the post office centennial celebration, 1982.

Releasing Balloons at Post Office Centennial Celebration, April 24, 1982.

The town held a Centennial Celebration for the local post office which was established August 24, 1882. The celebration was held on Saturday, April 24, 1982, in front of the post office building located at 24 Carrollton Street. This building is now known as the Otwell Building and is the social hall for the Temple United Methodist Church.

The program consisted of speeches, music, and a social hour. Hugh Hudsputh, postmaster, was presented with a certificate by Rick Palmer, a postal service coordinator. The certificate bears the names of all postmasters and postmistresses who have served here. It hangs in the post office today. At the conclusion of the outdoor affair, 100 red, white, and blue helium-filled balloons were released by senior citizens.

A new United States Post Office was completed in May 1991, at 68 James Street. Currently, ten rural routes serving 6,105 deliveries cover 543 miles. Eight hundred sixty seven post office boxes have been issued.

Many messages of both sadness and joy have been delivered by the local postal employees since it all began here in 1882.

CHAPTER XIII

INDUSTRY

The chief manufacturing in Temple for much of its history has been the production of wood products.

The first such factory was Stevens Manufacturing Company which was founded April 26, 1926 by L.A., Milton, Allen and Lawrence T. Stevens on West Johnson Street at Bell Street. L.E.C. (Allen) Stevens purchased the interest of his partners and operated the business until 1962. The company made screen doors, windows, dinette suites, and cabinets. The three story building had 75,000 square feet of floor space which included an open elevator which was used to carry materials from floor to floor. The company's whistle blew each working day to announce work time, lunch hour, and quitting time. This business made the auditorium seats for the 1939 Sage Street School. After being sold to Parrish Cabinet Company of Center Point, the building was consumed in a tremendous fire in 1966.

Stevens Manufacturing Company, 1953

Dave Williams Manufacturing Company

East Johnson Street at Rome Street

The Temple Furniture and Novelty Company was established by Roy B. Manning in 1932. The company made breakfast room suites, cabinets, and children's tables and chairs. It was located on East Johnson Street at Rome Street.

D.C. Williams also had a furniture manufacturing company in Temple for a number of years. During World War II, when metal was scarce, his plant made wooden wagons for children.

In the 1940s, the Temple Hosiery Mill was operated in the building next to the pharmacy by Winfred Smith.

J.A. Bowles operated a furniture factory in the old schoolhouse at the corner of James and Griffin Streets. He later added another building. The company was known as C&B Furniture Company. Its products included cabinets, breakfast room suites, chiffoniers, and chairs. In the 1950s, Bowles sold to Stylecrest, makers of early American living room furniture. Mrs. Frankie Tally was a partner in the firm. Stylecrest later sold to Temple Manufacturing Company owned by Homer Williams, William P. Johnson, and Brown Stevens.

In 1953, a branch of Roy Sewell Manufacturing Company of Bremen located in Temple. The men's suit manufacturer occupied its new plant on West Johnson Street. Men's pants were made here after being cut out in Bowdon Junction, and then they were carried to Bremen where the coat division of the company was located. Sewell's was the largest employer here for many years. The plant employed about 200 people.

The aforementioned Parrish Cabinet Company, owned by Roy Parrish, made china cabinets, tables, and chairs at their Center Point location for several decades.

Unfortunately, all of the above manufacturing concerns are no longer operating. This, of course, is emblematic of manufacturing across the nation. However, new industries are finding Temple attractive for business.

In 1972, Temple Wood Products, Inc., a division of Baker Industries, built a plant on West Sage Street. Wooden cable reels were manufactured there. In 1979, it was sold to Sonoco of Hartsville, S.C. Today, it is a service center for Sonoco reels.

West Georgia Bridge and Crown Lab was established by Lester Harmon along with partner Don Harmon in 1974 on Sage Street at Wells Avenue.

Lee Fabricators, established in 1978 on Hwy 113 north of Morgan Road, provides structural steel components to the recreation, food service, and cryogenics industries. This facility is the sole maker of handlebars for Harley-Davidson motorcycles assembled in North America.

Temple Industrial Park is a 102-acre site just south of Interstate 20. Carroll Tomorrow and the Carroll County Chamber of Commerce have been instrumental in developing this site. Janus International, a maker of roll-up doors, was the first tenant. It employs more than three hundred people. Royal Metal Products, manufacturer of special duct work, is also located in the park. On January 28, 2011, the park was named a Georgia Ready for Accelerated Development (GRAD) site, one of only fifteen such sites in Georgia.

CHAPTER XIV

BANKING

Banking had its beginning here when the Temple Banking Company opened for business in 1903 at the corner of West Johnson and Rome Streets. J. Frank Durrett was the first cashier. Among the other cashiers at later dates were A.K. Snead, H. Kimbrough, and L.F. West.

In 1913, the bank built a gleaming yellow-brick building at the corner of James and Sage. The building is now occupied by Temple Pharmacy. Farmers State Bank was housed in a building on Sage near the center of the store fronts. J.G. Smith and J.F. Hamilton were among the cashiers. The antiquated bank vault still remains in this building.

The banks flourished, as did the entire town, when Temple was at the center of a large and prosperous cotton market. However, as business slowed in the 1920s and approached the depression of the 1930s, the banks were forced to close.

Temple was without a bank until July 7, 1947, when the Bank of Temple opened for business in the former Farmers State Bank building. The bank brought to Temple the chance to locally finance homes, businesses, crops, and automobiles in addition to other types of loans. Dave Williams was the first president. He was followed by Dr. C.R. Hart, J.H. Thomas, and Mrs. C.R. Hart. Mr. N. Roma Henderson was the first cashier. After he retired in 1950, L.G. Lyell became cashier.

Among those serving as directors were: C.R. Hart, Dave Williams, Roy B. Manning, Euell West, Claude M. Morris, J.H. Thomas, C.A. Truitt, G.M. Burns, Mrs. C.A. Truitt, Mrs. C.R. Hart, and L.G. Lyell. Mr. Lyell served as Vice President and cashier until his retirement in 1970.

In October 1969, the outstanding stock of the bank was purchased by C.A. Roush and Associates of Carrollton. The Bank of Temple became the Bank of Carroll County. A beautiful building designed by Roy Denney and Associates was built at the corner of the Sage and Carrollton Streets on the site of the old Fowler Warehouse in 1971. Branches were located in Villa Rica in 1974, Bowdon in 1978, and Whitesburg in 1979. Assets grew from one million dollars in 1969 to sixteen million by 1982. The building now serves as the City Hall.

The Bank of Carroll County, which originally opened in 1947 as Bank of Temple became Citizens Bank and Trust on October 1, 1985. A new building was built at the south corner of Highway 78 and Carrollton Street. It became the Bank of North Georgia on October 27, 2008. Several banks in the area did not survive the economic recession. First National Bank of Georgia, which opened at the north corner of Carrollton Street and Hwy 78 in September 2000, was closed by federal regulators on January 29, 2010, and reopened the next day as Community & Southern Bank. Subsequently, the parent company closed this branch location in December 2012.

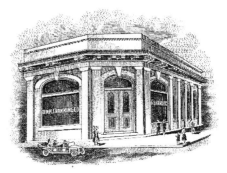

Temple Banking Company

CHAPTER XV

ORGANIZATIONS
1982 Reprint

Temple Masonic Lodge. Temple Masonic Lodge No. 322 was chartered October 27, 1886. The upper story of the two-story, frame schoolhouse was the meeting place. The Lodge owned the second floor of the building.

Early Masters were: William Brooks, J.W. Allgood, R.L. Rowe, W.L. Rowe, R.W. West, W. B. Chandler, D. H. Hamrick, T. S. West, Z.T. Adams, C.E. Ringer, and C.T. Stallings.

Other Masters included: W.T. Lambert, L.L. Birch, B.W. Treadaway, C.E. Stallings, C.D. Dewberry, L.F. West, R.O. Muse, W.L. Adcock, G.D. Jacobs, G.C. Ringer, W.L. Raburn, R.B. Manning, W.F. Lambert, M.L. Lamar, C.R. Hart, J.L. Carroll, O.E. Lewis, W.H. Shepard, J.D. Yeager, G.F. Moore, J.W. Hixon, G.P. Lamar, J.O. Lee, G.W. Cole, L.C. Bradley, F.W. Ivey, W.R. Glasscock, H.C. Holloman, E.E. Head, S.R. Stovall, J.C. Dobbs, Jr., H.A. Allgood, R.H. Gordon, O.R. Tuggle, B.E. Williams, R.D. Simpkins, Sr., L.C. Waddell, N.T. Robinson, Johnny Hopson, Henry Nordholm, Carl Maples, and Sammy Rogers.

In 1903, the Lodge purchased the back portion of the second floor of the Griffin building at the corner of James and Sage Streets. On September 12, 1959, the Lodge held its first meeting at its new Masonic Hall on the corner of James and Tallapoosa Streets.

Temple Chapter No. 495, Order of Eastern Star. The Temple Masonic Lodge invited an order of the Eastern Star Chapter to organize here. A group met on May 2, 1960, for the purpose of organizing this chapter.

The Masons chose to call this chapter West Chandler, in honor of Thomas S. West and William B. Chandler who had been dedicated, faithful members to this lodge down through the years. The name was changed to Temple Chapter in 1980.

This chapter was instituted on May 15, 1960, with thirty-two members. Mrs. Edith Jacobs, daughter of Bro. John West, was elected to serve as first worthy matron. Bro. Hugh Shepard served as first worthy patron.

On December 4, 1960, West Chandler Chapter was constituted with Grand Officers presiding and given the number 495.

The following have served as worthy matrons: Edith Jacobs, Irma Lee, Lois Moore, Elizabeth DeFoor, Mary C. Cole, Lavonia Carroll, Mary Ella Hamrick, Eunice Craft, Polly Stallings, Elizabeth Evans, Mary Beth Morris, Betty Ashworth, Ethel Wright, Margie Eiland, Deborah Hare, Vicki Stovall, and Linda Eason.

Worthy patrons have been Hugh Shepard, James O. Lee, George Moore, Herman Martin, Gordon Cole, Lawrence Stephens, Harvey Craft, Lowell Waddell, Paul Evans, A.G. Ashworth, Johnny Wright, A.C. Eiland, John R. Johnson, Steve Stovall, and James L. Eason.

Buck Creek Masonic Lodge. Lodge No. 639 was chartered October 29, 1913. Until 1927, the Masters were D.R. Brock, O.L. Hammond, F.J. Cole, W.H. Spence, W.E. Boen, and J.F. Cole. The lodge meets at the Pleasant Ridge Church. D.R. Brock wrote *"Brock's Manual."* It is still used today in many lodges as a guideline for Masons. Since 1913, a supper serving chicken stew and oyster stew has been held on the first Saturday night in April.

Masters since 1927: Aubrey Brock, C.W. Shadrix, A.D. Muse, Robert Cole, T.N. Bearden, Roy McKenzie, H. M. Shadrix, W.B. Norman, Jack Newsome, Joe Brand, Lindsey West, Dewey Caldwell, Billy Baxter, H.O. Burt, James S. Couch, Sam Green, Ralph Griffin, Bobby Holcombe, Harry Hughes, Jimmy Redding, Robert Redding, Kenneth Shadrix, J.G. McCalman, Hiram McKenzie, T.I. Mote, C.H. Spence, R.L. Cole, O.L. Stamps, S.W. Driver, W.M. Eidson, J.P. Baxter, Joe Bonner, Larry Jennings, Billy White, Gordon Sharp, David Caldwell, J.N. Baxter, and Hollis Hand.

Independent Order of Odd Fellows. Records of I.O.O.F. Lodge No. 122 of Temple were not located. This group is a benevolent fraternal organization much like the Masons. The group met in the two-story frame schoolhouse building built in 1888. The Odd Fellows were the nation's largest fraternal organization in the period 1870-1910.

**Lodge Hall, Temple Academy Building,
Late 1800s, Independent Order of Oddfellows**

Major Temple Garden Club. The club was organized June 4, 1935, and was affiliated with the Garden Clubs of Georgia in January 1937. The meeting date was set as the second Thursday of each month. The constitution, by-laws and rules of the club were drawn up and adopted. They remain in effect as originally written. The first president was Mrs. H.H. Sewell. Others were: Mesdames C.R. Hart, W.L. Steadham, Sr., W.L. Adcock, G.M. Burns, C.A. Truitt, D.F. Staples, L.B. McBrayer and Ruby Reeves.

Through the years, the club has had many interesting programs and distinguished speakers; it has staged many flower shows and sponsored many projects. Among them were planting dogwoods, crepe myrtles, and roses in town and on Bankhead Highway, and the erection and maintenance of the Chapel at Asbury Cemetery.

The twenty-fifth and fortieth anniversaries of the club were celebrated with open house at which neighboring clubs and friends were in attendance. The club was named for Major Temple, Chief Engineer of the Georgia Pacific Railroad.

Boy Scouts. The Boy Scout Troop received its charter in January, 1938 as Troop No. 11. I.S. Ingram was among the speakers when the charter was presented. John McGukin was the scoutmaster. The members were Elvin Dewberry, Edward Morris, Emmett Mathews, J.T. Hixon, Earl Robinson, J.P. Rowe, Harrison Stallings, Raymond Teel, and J.D. Wester, Jr.

Some years later a group was reorganized as Troop 96. Scoutmasters have been: Byron Lambert, W.T. Raburn, Ralph Dewberry, G.P Lamar, Charles Thomas, Sr., Bill West, Bobby Gentry, Tim Bass, and Richard Bracknell.

Donald Allgood was the first member to achieve the rank of Eagle Scout in Temple. Others who also reached this rank were: Robert McBrayer, Charles Thomas Jr., Earnest Buttram, Ned Hamil, Bobby Bolden, Johnny Baxter, and Mike Allgood. This high rank was awarded posthumously to William McColister, son of Homer and Morine McColister. Larry Huckeba attained the rank of Eagle Scout at Center Point.

Under the leadership of Richard Bracknell, the following became Eagle Scouts in 1974: Allan Gentry, Dave Stitcher, Terry Shadrix, Scott Holder, Charles Kelley, and David Stephens.

Various outstanding community services were performed as part of the requirements in attaining the rank of Eagle. The boys worked cooperatively on each other's projects. The group raised the funds and installed the first street signs in Temple in the summer of the bicentennial year. This was the project of David Stephens and was accomplished with the assistance of the city.

In 1959, a scout hut was built on the edge of the school grounds. Johnny Baxter and Charles Thomas, Jr. received the God and Country Award from Temple Methodist Church. Charles Thomas Sr., scoutmaster, received the Silver Beaver Award in 1963. In 1964, Charles Thomas Jr. and his father, scoutmaster Charles Thomas, Sr., attended the national Boy Scout Jamboree at Valley Forge, Pennsylvania. In the same year, Charles Thomas, Jr. presented the Georgia Scouting report to Governor Carl Sanders. The Temple Masonic Lodge has sponsored the troop since its beginning.

Dayton Crawford attained the rank of Eagle Scout in 1981.

Men's Civic Clubs. The Chamber of Commerce was an active service organization in the 1950s. It was followed by the Ruritan Club. Both clubs carried out worthwhile services for the town. In 1976, the Temple Lions Club was organized at Treasure Lake Country Club. The new club was sponsored by the Bremen Lions Club. Claude Parrish was elected as the first president. Since 1976, Jim McWilliams, Max Conner, Gene Yearty, Nolan Cheek, and Johnny Hopson have served as president.

CHAPTER XVI

CHURCHES

This chapter was written in 1982 to capture the early histories of area churches. Only a few minor changes have been made. In the past several decades, new churches or additions have been built to accommodate growth, while some established churches relocated. Some are meeting in storefront buildings awaiting an improved economy to build. However, they all continue to meet the needs of the community.

Our Lady of Perpetual Help. The church is located on a thirteen-acre site on Center Point Road. The church was constructed in 1962 to meet the spiritual needs of an expanding Catholic population in this area.

It is a structure of contemporary design, its exterior of Stone Mountain granite and redwood siding with amber glass windows. Over the main entrance a slender silver cross soars above an aluminum and mosaic mural symbolizing Christ's title, "The Divine Word Made Flesh." Some 550 residents of Carroll and Haralson counties comprise the parish family as of 1982.

Catholics have worshipped in several locations in this area of West Georgia since before the turn of the century. Their first church was a former one-room schoolhouse in a settlement near Tallapoosa named Budapest. Homemade benches, bare kneelers, and a pot-bellied stove provided a measure of comfort for the 200 families, mostly of Hungarian ancestry, who were summoned to Mass by the old school bell. Under the guidance of Father Francis Janishek, the church and the little community of Budapest flourished. Vineyards were planted by the settlers, migrants in 1893 from the mining regions of Pennsylvania. A wine-making industry was begun, and the success of the venture soon attracted migrants from Ohio and various other sections of the nation. A second township, Nitra, was formed by a colony of Slovakian ancestry. It prospered and grew into a community of sixty buildings including a Catholic church and rectory, stores, and a post office. Grapevines blanketed the hills, storage vats were in use, and wineries were planned.

The promising new wine-making industry was destined for failure, however, for the State Prohibition Act of 1907 put an end to the hopes of the settlers. To find new sources of income, one by one, they were forced to move away. The few Catholic families who remained were served by mission priests who, for fifty-five years, traveled from Rome and Atlanta, by horse and buggy and Model T, to say Mass – in private homes, in a traveling chapel, and in the old schoolhouse.

With industrial growth and development of the West Georgia area, the Catholic population again began to grow. By the early 1950s, a number of Catholic families were living in the vicinity, some of them traveling as far as thirty miles to Budapest for Sunday services. The need for a more centrally located church became urgent.

In November 1952, the Episcopal Church on South White Street in Carrollton, a historical landmark dating back to 1893, was offered for sale. With the approval of the Most Rev. Francis E. Hyland, Bishop of Atlanta, who made the first payment, the handful of parishioners set to work to raise funds for the purchase. Through local money-making projects and substantial donations from the Catholic Extension Society of Chicago and from friends in West Georgia and Atlanta, the financial goal was reached. The parish took possession of the church on August 1, 1953.

The little church met the immediate needs of its members, but soon the continually growing Catholic community needed a larger, more modern church home. On September 30, 1961, Bishop Hyland approved construction of a new parish plant on the spacious site just off the Carrollton-Temple Road for the members of Our Lady of Perpetual Help Church. The following spring, on

March 25, 1962, a Solemn High Mass was celebrated and the newly constructed church blessed. For the first time in local Catholic history, the parish family had a home which was theirs from its inception.

The church was built with an eye to the future but retains touches of a humbler past. Heirlooms included in the furnishings are an antique lamp in the vestibule from the Carrollton church and the Stations of the Cross which once hung in the old church in Budapest. The new building has continuous arches and columns of laminated pine and ceiling of British Columbia pine. The altar is translucent white Alabama marble, the crucifix sculpted in Italy, and baldacchino designed by noted artist Joel Reeves hangs over it.

The property was donated by Mr. and Mrs. F. Eaton Chalkley. Both Mr. Chalkley and his wife, Susan Hayward, were leading figures in construction of the church. Susan Hayward was a famous, most talented movie actress and recipient of an Academy Award in 1958.

The Chalkleys moved from Carroll County in 1964. In 1966, Mr. Chalkley died and was buried alongside the church. The memorial at the site was designed by his wife. On March 14, 1975, Susan Hayward Chalkley died. Her body rests at the side of Eaton, beneath an image of the agonizing Head of the Crucified Christ, recessed in the center of the memorial.

Center Point Methodist Church. The first Methodist church in this community was located one mile northwest of the present location at Center Point. It was known as County Line Methodist Church and was established in the early 1800s.

At a conference at County Line in 1903, permission was granted to build a new church at Center Point. The building committee included J.D. Wester, T.E. Bartlett, and Giles McCullough. When the church was finished it was valued at $1,000. Land was donated by Wesley Dominick. Land for the cemetery was given by Mary Ophelia McCullough, Z.L. Levans, and Cecil Levans, in three different portions at different dates.

Charter members were J.T. Bonner, Rhuey M. Levans, James D. Wester, Alice A. Crockett, John H. Bartlett, Mary O. McCullough, Harry Crockett, Lela Crockett, Mary Bartlett, Sarah Crockett, Ophie Bartlett, Eddie Bonner, R.R. Ballard, T.E. Bartlett, Marvin Wester, Samuel Haynes, Lucy B. Wester, Ira W. Witcher, Effie Ola Haynes, Alice Haynes, W. Gordon Bartlett, Clark Bartlett, Mattie Bartlett, and Melissa E. Witcher.

The church won first place in the Rome District in a Town and Country Development Program in 1952-1953. Rev. Herschel Sheets was pastor and many improvements were made in the physical and spiritual structure.

No major changes were made in the building until 1949 when a vestibule and two Sunday School rooms were added. New memorial windows, a new chancel rail and new pews were installed. A rock entrance was also built. In 1958, an educational building was erected.

Center Point was on the Carrollton Circuit until 1947 when it was changed to the Temple Circuit. This circuit included Center Point, Temple, and Concord. Center Point had Sunday worship services once each month. In 1959, the church went to half time with Concord and remained this way until 1975 when, under the leadership of Rev. Ferrell Drummond, the church became full time.

In June 1975, Max Caylor, a student at Emory University, was assigned as the first full time pastor.

The Church at Carrollton (formerly **Abilene Baptist Church**). On May 8, 1875, twenty-six Baptists met at the home of Sef Muse and organized the Abilene Baptist Church. The church first met under a bush arbor. The following charter members made up the organization: Benjamin Creel,

J.H. Haynes, Z.W. Muse, D.W. Gray, G.F. Spence, John Akin, J.D. Morgan, H.B. Bartlett, W.L. Dodson, J.G. Fernanda, B.S. Tillman, J.M. Muse, John Keys, R.A. Stephens, Sarah Creel, Corsinda Haynes, E.A. Muse, Sarah Akins, Lucy D. Morgan, Mary J. Bartlett, Isabelle Dodson, Elizabeth Tillman, Amanda Meadows, M.E. Muse, Nancy Keyes, and Mary Stephens.

Construction of the first church building was begun in 1892. It was a small unceiled building near the road in front of the present church. Mrs. Elmira Muse, a charter member, cooked dinner and walked over a mile to carry the men their lunch. She was honored by the church when she was 100 years old. She lived to be 105.

In 1902, foot washing was abolished. The first singing school, taught by Jim Hixon, was held. Bob Hendon was the chorister.

In 1938-1939, six Sunday School rooms were built. During the period of 1940-1948, the church was brick veneered, a vestibule was added, and new pews were purchased. Memorial windows were also added. Mr. and Mrs. T.N. Bearden supplied the pulpit in memory of their son, Eckert, who was the only member who lost his life during World War II.

In 1946, D.A. (Dan) Jackson gave a barbecue in honor of the boys returning from World War II. This event was held at his farm in the pasture. The barbecue was such a success that it became an annual custom. It is held each year in August. For several years it was held in the homes of different families, but for the last several years it has been on the church grounds. It has never been rained out since its beginning in 1946.

Improvements have been made at the church through the years. Sunday School rooms have been added several times. In 1959, the church voted to hold full time services. A pastorium was built in 1963 and in 1971 a fellowship hall was constructed.

A bus ministry was begun in 1972. The next year Mr. and Mrs. Hoyatt Reid presented an organ to the church in memory of Terry Rogers. Dewey Caldwell, who began his music ministry at the age of twelve, held the position of chorister for more than forty years.

Pleasant Ridge Baptist. In 1894, with the help of Abilene and Pleasant View Churches, the Pleasant Ridge Baptist Church was constituted under a bush arbor. In 1895, the church was admitted to the Carrollton Baptist Association. The church had seventeen members.

A plank building was erected in 1905. The pews were put together with wooden pegs. The building which is used today was built in 1915. Sunday School rooms were added in 1948. A complete renovation of the sanctuary was accomplished in 1950. In 1975, four Sunday School rooms were added and a church library was started.

Bethel Baptist. The church was constituted June 26, 1854, with sixteen charter members. They were: Merriman and Harreeth Stephens, James and Caroline Raburn, John P. Echols, John and Mary Muse, John, Jane, and Sara Riggs, William, Mary and Susan Morgan, Elizabeth Barfield, James and Caroline Pace. The present property was deeded to the deacons of the church on September 12, 1854. Rev. W.M. Wood was the first pastor.

In 1960, the present church building was erected. Sunday School rooms have been added several times. A bus ministry is responsible for a large increase in Sunday School enrollment and attendance. The church is located about three miles south of Temple on Hwy 113.

Concord Primitive Baptist. This church is located on Hwy 113 in the Abilene community. It is one of the oldest in the county, having been organized in 1834. The church once stood about one mile northwest of the present structure. The old cemetery marks the spot of the original site.

Some of the first members were the Reids, Upshaws, Coles, Chandlers, and Holcombs.

Concord Methodist. In 1828, one year after Carroll County was established, Concord Methodist Church was constituted with thirteen charter members. James Baskin was instrumental in establishing the church. He came to this section of Carroll County to homestead, and gave land for the first meeting house. The first building was erected the same year. It was of logs and was eighteen feet square.

James Baskin recorded in his diary that it was the dream of the charter members that the people of the area would live in love and harmony. They named the church Concord in hopes his dream would be borne out.

Among charters members were Allen, Baxter, Bryce, Cash, Powell, Taylor, Turner, Wynn, and Ballard.

Concord, through the circuit rider system and local preachers, was the mother of many local Methodist churches in the county. Powell's Chapel and Smyrna are among the churches which were begun as outreaches from Concord.

The organization of the first Methodist Church in Brazil traces its history to missionaries, Mr. and Mrs. Alfred I. Smith, who were Concord members who left for that country in 1869. In 1870, in the yard of Mr. and Mrs. Smith, Bishop Pierce held the first Conference in Brazil and organized officially the Methodist Church there.

Records list the following local preachers as being leaders in early Methodism in Carroll County and surrounding areas: James Baskin, James Bryce, James Stripling, David Stripling, William Brooks, William Francis Spaight Powell, Levi Thomas Gardner Powell, J.F. Bryce, Biyed Kelley, Jesse Garrison, and Sam Baskin.

The second church building was constructed in 1836, also of logs and twenty-four feet square. The third house was a frame building and was built in 1854 as a cost of about $500. The fourth church was built in 1891. The present building was constructed in 1909 after a storm wrecked the former building. The building, costing $4,000, was dedicated by Bishop Warren A. Candler. The Church School Annex was completed in 1954. Through the years, the buildings have always been rebuilt on the same location. The cornerstone marking the original property line laid out by James Baskin in 1828 remains as he erected it.

In the early years, the church was served by circuit riders who came to preach every six to eight weeks. During the absence of the circuit rider, the spiritual life of the church was carried on by local preachers, unordained men who could "exhort" but could not serve the sacraments, and by class leaders who organized study groups on the meaning of Christian living. They met in homes of members.

Sabbath School was begun in 1868. The Women's Missionary Society started in the mid-1890s with Mollie Wynn as the first president.

In the 1860s, twenty-four African-American members were listed on the roll. From this group emerged an outstanding minister, Rev. Larkin Walker, who preached at Concord to the African-American congregation and to other congregations in surrounding areas. He is buried at Concord.

In 1865, during the worst of the Civil War, Concord was without a pastor for the only time in its history. The records indicate that through local preachers and class leaders the spiritual life of the church and community was maintained.

In the early years, following the "laying by" of crops, great revivals were held at Concord. This tradition is kept alive today, for the third week in August is still set aside for revivals. One of the high moments in the history of the church was in August of 1896 when fifty-four persons were received into the church on one day during the revival. Rev. W.T. Irvine was pastor.

From 1928 until 1975, the church was part of a circuit, sharing the minister with another church. At times, Concord has been grouped with the congregation of Villa Rica, Temple, and Carrollton. In 1956, the church was paired with Center Point. In 1975, the local membership voted to withdraw from the circuit and to support its own ministry.

New Canaan Baptist. The church was organized in 1881 with the assistance of Flat Rock Baptist Church of Villa Rica. Among the deacons as of 1982 have been Nick New, F.C. Elam, Wiley Bohanan, William Strickland, William Harris, Charlie Bassett, Robert Hammock, C.C. Greenwood, Jake Garrett, G.W. Johnson, G.W Perkins, John Dobbs, John Scales, G. F. Johnson, Donn Powell, Rufus Rowe, Luther Houston, Bud McKinley, Ermus Perkins, Clifford I. Barnes, Ray Scales, Leonard Gray, Hugh Hall, Wesley Phillips and Jimmie Dobbs.

Among the clerks as of 1982 have been Bud Stone, C.C. Greenwood, Samuel Sims, and E.B. Elliott. Some of the missionary workers have been Eliza New, Vina Elam, Mary Elliott, Louise Harris and Ella Elam.

Among those who have served as pastors as of 1982 are Dan Maddox, Hobb Style, Jim Roberson, T.M. Hammock, A.J. Beavers, Rev. Maxwell, G.W. Luke, J.T. Trice, F.M. Hutchinson, B.J. Jackson, E.W. Willis, C.L. Nalls and W.M. Calhoun.

In 1963, a new church was built near the old one on Rome Street.

New Brooklyn Baptist. The New Brooklyn Church was organized in 1931 with forty-seven members. Since that time, Sunday School rooms have been added and the church has been bricked.

Among the pastors as of 1982 have been W.M. Williams, J. W. Holland, W. F. Lassetter, James Crabb, Grover Cook, Buddy York, Ralph Tapley, L.D. Palmer, Roy King, C.L. Lyles, Willie Hammond, Thomas Garner, J.O. Weaver, and A.M. Ballenger.

Temple Church of Christ. Family worship service in the home of George Scott in 1946 was the beginning of the Temple Church of Christ. Hedric Laney and his family joined the Scotts in 1949. In 1952, a tent meeting was held by Minister Homer L. King. The Joe Bass family joined at this time. The group of worshipers started holding meetings in the old Temple Theater building.

The modern brick structure at the corner of Griffin and James Streets was built over a period of time as funds became available. Hedric Laney and Joe Bass served as trustees. Among the ministers as of 1982 have been Homer A. Gay, Gillis Prince, E.H. Miller, Alton Bailey, T.J. Parker, Barry Owens, and Dennis Smith.

Griffin Chapel United Methodist. Griffin Chapel is a daughter church of Welcome Chapel Church which first located at Mandeville Mill, Carroll County.

Welcome Chapel was started by Zach Vaughn, Green Vaughn, and Rev. Billy Ables. Its first pastor was Rev. Zachriah Vaughn. This was many years before the establishment of the Rome District or a African-American district superintendent.

Later, the brush arbor church moved to Center Point. Then, the next property purchased by the people for worshipping purposes consisted of a frame house on West Johnson Street in Temple. The Griffins wanted the property so a fair exchange was made for the present site where Griffin Chapel now stands. The small, yet growing band moved into a newly erected building and changed its name to Griffin Chapel, under the pastorate of Rev. Zachriah Vaughn.

On August 11, 1894, Griffin Chapel became a charter member of the Epworth League of the Methodist Episcopal Church, Rome District, Savannah Conference.

As of 1982, among the ministers of the church have been N.J. Ross, W.C. Bryant, A.J. Booth, J.W. Spencer, J.H. Brandon, G.W. Hatcher, P.B. Gates, Z.K. Gowen, W.C. Von Shultz, A.C. Cobb, J.H. Bridges, Rev. Dorsey, Rev. Swain, Rev. Beasely, E.G. Hinton, S. Clark, W.B. Burton, M.S. Moore, J.C. Collier, Rev. Taggart, Rev. Kimball, B.F. Griggs, and W.E. Mackey.

In 1948, Rev. E.G. Hinton envisioned a new structure for Griffin Chapel. He, along with the laity of the church, started a building fund. The present structure was completed in 1966.

On October 9, 2005, a new building, "The Wholeness Center," was dedicated, and the church observed its 135th anniversary under the direction of Rev. Bobby Church.

First Baptist Church of Temple. The Temple Baptist Church was organized November 1, 1884, with fifteen charter members: J.M. Daniel, S.B.L.J. McClung, J.M.D. Stallings, J.V. Riggs, Marthia Daniel, Deborah McClung, Mary E. Stallings, A.V. Riggs, Sarah Crocket, Amanda Jones, Sophronia Stallings, Hariette Vandergriff, Margret Vandergriff, Susan Phillips, and Anna Vandergriff.

The first church building was a wooden structure located several yards west of the present church site. The present brick building was erected in the early 1900s. Modifications of the sanctuary and building of annexes have been accomplished during the years. Memorial windows and other items have been given to the church through the years in memory of loved ones. The most recent were chimes. They were given to the church in memory of Roy B. Manning, church chorister for many years, by his family and friends. In 1975, the name of the church was changed to First Baptist Church of Temple.

The pastors of the church have been J.M.D. Stallings, A.J. Coalson, W.W. Roop, T.A. Howard, J.W. Maltbie, J.W. Griffith, W.A. Davis, H.H. Connell, W.R. Barrow, J.M. Spinks, T.R. Morgan, G.W. Jones, W.P. Cumbie, B.W.J. Graham, H.B. Reynolds, Monroe Burns, Jimmy Burnham, Carl N. Tapley, Elwood Cline, Harry Brazell, Carl Billue, Allen Martin, Glenn Clonts, Mike Mims and the present pastor, Larry Boswell.

In 2007, a family activity center, which included a youth classroom, was constructed.

Mount Carmel Baptist Church. It is believed that the Mt. Carmel Church was first established between 1871 and 1878 as a Methodist Church. It also served as a schoolhouse. It was later changed over to a New Hope Baptist and then to Missionary Baptist which it is today. The building burned in the early 1920s and was rebuilt in 1926. It was still used as a schoolhouse. Mr. and Mrs. Leonard McBrayer were among those who taught there in the 1930s.

Mr. McBrayer's grandfather, Andrew E. McBrayer, donated the land for the church site. Mrs. McBrayer's grandfather preached the first sermon in the church. In 1925, Brother Palmer, a New Hope Baptist preacher, became the pastor. It is not known exactly when it was changed to Missionary Baptist.

Among the charter members after the church was reorganized in 1929 were: Mr. and Mrs. Y.B. Ragsdale, C.B. Shirah, W.L. Adcock, Mrs. Lula Rainey, Mr. and Mrs. Leonard McBrayer, Sharon Ragsdale, Louise Ragsdale, Mrs. Rena Chance, C.B. White, Elma Ingram, Nannie Ingram, George Hansen, Fannie Hansen, S.M. Rutledge, J.D. Braswell, E.W. Ivey, T.J. Womack, Olin Johnson, Verlie Chance, Clyde Holloman, W.R. Shackleford, Carrie L. Womack, Martell Rutledge, Ovie Hansen, Mamie Bentley, W.T. Durrett, Ralph Durrett, Felton Chapman, Mr. and Mrs. W.Z. Shackleford, N.R. Shirah, Mrs. Vivian Chance Norton, G.O. Carroll, and Lottie Bell Chance.

Among the pastors as of 1982 are Y.B. Ragsdale, W.O. Cook, E.J. Cain, J.W. Womack, J.C. Pace, Roy Stanford, Tag Holland, Cliff Tyson, W.J. Jenkins, F.L. Carter, Artis Busbin, Grover

Sheets, Thomas Garner, Charles Williams, C.L. Lyles, Clarence Agan, Curtis Cole, Jesse Robinson, Hiram McKenzie, and Carlin Phillips.

Temple United Methodist Church. Asbury Church, the direct predecessor of the Temple United Methodist Church, was built in 1857 or 1858 across the road from Asbury Cemetery. It was a wooden structure named for one of Methodism's early bishops, Francis Asbury. Trustees at its inception were Wilson Cartwright, Warren Chance, Jesse Cantrell, and Andrew McColister.

In 1884, Temple Methodist Church was established. A wooden structure was built on the present site, and the membership included the seventy-two members from Asbury Church. Nineteen additional members were added that year.

During the summer of 1897, the church was so badly damaged by a windstorm that rebuilding was necessary. In 1898, the present building, the oldest brick church in the county, was erected. Jeff Johnson was in charge of brick laying. According to tradition, a school boy, Hamp Crawford, wanted a part in building the church. While workmen were away one noon, he laid three bricks his own way in the gable end of the structure.

Trustees when the present church was built were P.I. Sewell, M.J. Baxter, W.A. Enterkin, J.M. Walker, C.W. Griffin, and B.J. McCain.

At that time, the church was on a charge with other area churches, including Old Villa Rica, New Villa Rica, and Concord. In 1920, the pastor commuted by train from Villa Rica. He sometimes walked over the dirt road, staying in the homes of members over the weekend.

When the county celebrated its centennial in 1927, a model of Temple Methodist Church was presented on a parade float as the county's oldest brick church.

In 1959, the church, which had been on a charge with Concord and Center Point, became a station church. In 1960, the church was selected as "Rural Church of the Year" in the North Georgia Conference.

Woodland Christian Camp. A little over 16 years ago, a campground for Christian camping activities was developed on forty acres near Oak Grove Road. The Center Point property was purchased in 1964. On October 1, 1968, the Georgia Christian Assembly and the United Christian Men became one group known as the Woodland Christian Camp. A chapel, dining hall, eleven cabins, and caretaker's home were soon built. In 1970, a swimming pool was added.

In 1971, Earl H. Hobson and family came to Woodland as camp coordinators. They had returned to the states from teaching and working in Christian churches in Kingston, Jamaica.

West Georgia Baptist Church. This church is located at 197 Highway 78. Bobby Jarrett is the pastor.

Oak Hill Church of God of Prophecy. This church, located at 560 Morgan Road, was organized in 1935 by James Ingram.

Faith Baptist Church. The church was organized on June 13, 1977, at the Old Pace's Store building at Mt. Carmel. There were fifteen charter members, and Thomas Garner was the first pastor. The members built a new church in the New Brooklyn Community in 1979.

Liberty Christian Church. This church, located at 1689 Liberty Church Road, was organized in 1870. In the early days, the congregation met under a large oak tree on the Holcomb farm. Three early ministers include Isham Hicks, John Matthews, and John Tillery. John Q. Adams donated the property where the church was built around 1901. Many additions and improvements were made through the years. A parsonage was built in 1959 on land that was donated by Col. Claude Driver. A major renovation took place in 1969. A new fellowship hall and Sunday School rooms were built in 1992.

Our Lady of Perpetual Help Catholic

Center Point United Methodist

The Church at Carrollton

Pleasant Ridge Baptist

Bethel Baptist

Concord Primitive Baptist

Concord United Methodist

New Canaan Baptist

New Brooklyn Baptist

Temple Church of Christ

Griffin Chapel United Methodist

Temple First Baptist

Mt. Carmel Baptist

Temple United Methodist

West Georgia Baptist

Faith Baptist

Liberty Christian

CHAPTER XVII

COMMUNITIES NEARBY

Although Temple has boundary lines, the town spills over the invisible lines and flows in all directions into the surrounding countryside. The nearby communities, as well as Temple, are located in the old farming region of northern Carroll County. Some of them are Mount Carmel, Brooklyn, Center Point, Abilene, and Hickory Level. In each community there were usually a blacksmith shop, cotton gin, gristmill, sawmill, syrup mill, general store, church, and a one-room school. Before the days of Rural Free Delivery, a post office was located in a home or store in most communities. Many of these post offices cannot be traced historically since time and circumstances caused quite frequent changes in both ownerships and locations. However, some lasted for years at one location under a single-family proprietorship.

All of this section of the county is actually only one community because the people's heritage and lifestyle are very much the same. The people are bound together through their affiliations with the same industries, businesses, schools, and churches. They are even more closely bound because of friendships and kinships; both of which draw communities together.

Courtesy, Mr. and Mrs. James B. Shirah

Rutledge Cotton Gin at Mt. Carmel, 1920s

Mount Carmel. This community is northeast of Temple. Today the place is marked only by the church. Fred Rutledge's grandfather, Thomas "Bud" Rutledge, operated a cotton gin there. It was hand fed. He also had a shop, grist mill, and sawmill.

Bud Rutledge also had a post office in a side room of his house. It was known as Berlene, Georgia.

After his death, Fred Rutledge's father, W. Oscar Rutledge, put up a gin in 1913 across the road from the first one.

The school was housed in the church. A Mr. Keyes taught there. He was the father of Evelyn Keyes, a star in the world-famous movie, "Gone with the Wind." Some of the other teachers were Frank Morris, John Brooks, Mattie Brooks, Murdock Thomasson, Mr. and Mrs. W.L. Adcock, Mr. and Mrs. Leonard McBrayer, James E. Ingram, and Ivey West.

Brooklyn. The community is located northeast of Temple. In 1900, W.A. Taylor operated a gin there. It was sold to J.J. Taylor who operated it until 1925. C.W. Taylor bought the gin in 1926 and ran it until 1957. The Taylor's Gin road got its name from this gin. It was situated on the west side of the road a few hundred yards from Rainey Rd. The Taylors also had a grist mill. In the 1930s, E.C. Karr built a small store there and operated it for some time.

Brooks School was located in the community and was named for the Brooks family, a pioneer family in the area. Brooks School was abandoned when the Brooklyn School was built in the early 1900s. The school was started after the close of the Temple Model School. Several small schools consolidated to form the new school. There were five teachers. Among them was Phil Campbell, Sr., who had taught at Temple Model School.

Brooklyn had debate, track, and baseball teams. The school became known as "Chigger Ridge" because it was built back in the pines where chiggers were plentiful. Another reminder of chiggers was the red suits worn by the baseball team.

The school flourished for awhile, but finally got into financial trouble and could not meet its obligations. The students returned to their former, one-room schools near their homes.

Other teachers at Brooklyn were: Danny Campbell, S.E. Morgan, M.C. Wiley, Oscar Smith, John Brooks, Sam Cown, Paul Cobb, Mrs. Myrtis Henry, W.L. Adcock, Miss Ruth Smith, A.B. Crews, and Miss Lucile Shockley.

Courtesy, Times-Georgian

Taylor's Gin, Circa, 1910

Hickory Level. Hickory Level is one of the oldest settled places in the county. The first settler was Rev. James Baskin in 1828. He cut and hewed the logs from which he built his home. The land was very level and covered with hickory trees. The two features became the name of the settlement, Hickory Level.

Rev. Baskin named the place. He also donated a beautiful plot of land for a Methodist church, cemetery, and school. The academy was one of the best in the county. Scholars came from all around to attend school there.

On October 20, 1837, a post office was established at Hickory Level. Rev. (Uncle Jimmie) Baskin was the first postmaster. The post office remained until 1901 when it was no longer needed due to Rural Free Delivery. A blacksmith shop, grist mill, sawmill, cotton gin, and two stores were there. The two-story, frame store building located at the crossroads was known as the Pierce and Baskin store.

Among the early settlers were David Stripling, James Stripling, and James Bryce, all ministers and successful farmers. Others were John Smith, Sloman Wynn, Rev. Thomas G. Powell, Uncle "Billy" Taylor, Ned Gresham, Larkin Allen, Alsymus Allen, Billy McCain, Baxters, and Jesse Gray. Long before the Civil War the land was settled for miles around.

The community had an Odd Fellow Hall and a lodge which was quite active.

In 1910, Dr. S. Frank Scales began medical practice at Hickory Level. His wife was the nurse. Since there were no hospitals in the area at the time, Dr. Scales performed surgery on kitchen tables in his patients' homes. He later opened an office on the second floor of the general store. This served as a hospital. Dr. Scales and his wife served the people of the area faithfully for many years.

Farmville-Abilene. Before the county was organized, Uncle Hiram Sharp settled between Abilene and Concord Primitive Baptist Church at Sharp's Creek. He acquired a large acreage. As times got hard or if he got in a tight for money, he would sell some of the land.

A Protestant Methodist Church and a good school were located there. L.C. McCalman and Joe Cobb taught there. There were no public schools then. The patrons paid a monthly tuition fee. Some of the people who lived nearby and sent their children to Farmville School were Hiram Spence, George F. Spence, Jeremiah Cole, Gilbert Cole, S.V. Cole, Robert Wright, Elijah McPherson, Mrs. Pollard, Daniels, Jones, Jackson, McKenzie, Jessie W. Muse, Doctor Kee, Mrs. Parrish, widow of Captain Parrish, David Hamrick, James Baxter, and Hugh McMullen.

Jeremiah Cole moved near Old Concord Church in the early 1800s and he acquired enough land for all twelve of his children to have a home. He and his family arrived there by wagon. They lived in the wagon until they could cut logs and build a cabin. They had to keep a fire burning at night to keep the wolves away. Wild turkeys and other wild game were all around.

Hiram Sharp sold land to Hiram Spence, Jessie Muse, Sef Muse, and others. Hiram Spence called the community together to request that they all live together in peace and harmony. He invited everyone to have prayer services in his home each Wednesday night. The different denominations took turns having charge of the services.

In order that the children would be closer to the school, Farmville was abandoned and Pine Grove was built near the location of Jack Newsome's farm. For part of a term, a fourteen-year-old boy, Leon Spence, taught there. He later graduated from Augusta Medical College at the head of his class. He was then only 21.

A post office was established at Abilene in 1894. James M. McCalman was the first postmaster. W.M. "Billy" Spence was the postmaster for awhile at his home. Later, Mrs. Leon Spence served as postmistress. The first mail carrier brought the mail in a two-wheel cart. He blew a whistle fashioned from a hickory stick to let the patrons know that the mail had arrived.

The road from Abilene westward is known as Hog Liver Road. Mrs. Iva Spence Hendrix related how the road got its name: "There was a man who lived on the road and was a good butcher. People from miles around would have him come help them on hog-killing day. All he would charge would be the livers. He would string them up on a stick and carry them home. That's how Hog Liver Road got its name."

A custom in the days when local Methodists worshipped at Farmville was the annual barbecue that was held there. This event was well attended. It was an event which offered a great time of fellowship.

Center Point Store, W.A. Almon, Owner, Circa 1903.
Homer Phillips, Roy Almon, Warren Crockett, Newt West and Grady Almon

Center Point-Horace. Many years ago, Center Point was the justices court ground for the Kansas district. The area was named for the state of Kansas. One of the first settlers in the early 1800s was Elijah McPherson. His home was near the headwaters of Buck Creek. He had a sawmill there. Lumber was carried on wagons from his mill for some twenty-five miles. The land was very productive, and there was an abundance of wild game and timber. Wess McKissack's mill was located on one prong of the headwaters of Buck Creek. The mill was later operated by Cole. H.P. Bartlett had a mill on another prong of the creek.

There was a post office established in the home of Charles W. Bonner in 1892. It was called Horace, Georgia. A grist mill and a ginnery were operated by John Bonner and Son. There was also a flourishing Bold Springs School. Plans were being made to establish a Sabbath School. John McGukin and D.T. Beall had just completed their beautiful homes in 1893. In the same year, John Bonner drove a herd of cattle to the Gate City where he sold them. This was the custom.

The mail was brought to Temple by a man in a gulley jumper. This was a two-wheel buggy with no top. It had one seat and a small flat on each side to haul things. Homer Wester walked to the post office to get the bi-weekly newspaper in order to keep up with the developments of the Spanish-American War.

Some of the earliest settlers were the Bartletts, Spences, Wests, Almons, Bells, Westers, Sharps, McGukins, and Grays.

Center Point was so named because of the five main roads which intersect there. M.E.V. Spence built a store there in 1894. The carpenters were paid 50 cents per day. The store was operated under the name of Spence and Muse. It was later Spence and McCalman. The general store sold such things as cloth, overalls, hats, scarves, gloves, plow handles, scrapes and wings, and groceries. Coffee was sold as whole beans which were ground at home. At one time there were two stores at Center Point.

The Temple Oil Company built a gin there on the R.W. West farm in the early 1900s. This is now known as the Lloyd Wester place. The gin was operated by William West and was powered by a waterwheel. The pond was on what is now the J.V. Hamrick place. The water ran through wooden troughs around a hill to get enough fall to run the waterwheel.

Center Point had a school for many years before its consolidation with Temple in 1929. Among the teachers were Professor Olin Teal, M.E.V. Spence, J.R. Spence, Mrs. L.M. Wester, and Mrs. Hoyt Raburn. In 1889, Professor J.R. Spence enrolled seventy-five pupils. In 1894, Professor J.R. Spence served in the Georgia House of Representatives.

The Bob Toombs Debating Society was organized on January 19, 1889. The members were: J.R. Spence, J.M. Crow, L.C. Spence, R.W. West, J.E. Levans, M.E.V. Spence, T.S. West, H.T. Sharp, D.R. Brock, A.A. West, G.D. Haynes, G.S. Stovall, G.M. Jones, W.B. Wester, J.M. Jones, E.M. Chappell, J.G. Henry, D.G. Awtry, G.M. Wester, S.O. Wester, W.J. Crawford, S.M. Haynes, M.J. Moore, J.O. Sharp, and Bhekley Drew. They met on Saturday nights and debated on such topics as Woman's Suffrage and other subjects pertaining to the times. Dues were five cents. A fine of five cents was the penalty for speaking out of turn. Ten cents was collected from those using obscene language.

In 1896, the Grady and Watson Debating Society was organized. In the 1930s, the community had a very active Home Demonstration Club. A clubhouse was built just off the church grounds on land donated by Z.L. Levans. The building was used as the Center Point voting precinct.

In 1937, rural electric lines reached the area. This brought about many home and farm improvements. C.H. Wester was one of the original members of the Board of Directors of Carroll Electric Membership Corporation.

The Community Improvement Club was started in 1949. The officers were Mrs. C.L. Levans, President; Sam Hathcock, Vice President; Mrs. Leonard Ivey, Secretary; and Mrs. Lucille Allen, Reporter. The club won first place in county competition in 1950. The scrapbook of this organization won first place in the state in 1951. The club served to inspire people to continually improve home and community life.

In 1950, there were forty boys and girls in 4-H Club work. In addition to meetings at school, they met weekly at the clubhouse. At the same time, Mr. and Mrs. Hoyt Raburn were the leaders of an active Cub Scout pack. The Boy Scouts were under the leadership of Donald Levans. A chapter of the Carroll County Farm Bureau was organized in 1950. In 1953, College in the Country was started with Collus Johnson as director. Many people from West Georgia College spoke to the group on subjects of interest.

The first hard-surfaced roads were built through Center Point in 1951.

The 1940s and 1950s were times of great change in agriculture. It was no longer profitable to raise cotton. The farmers adopted a diversified type farming which included raising pimento peppers. The community raised twenty-four tons of peppers in 1950. In the fall, a Pimento Festival was held in Carrollton. The float of Center Point won third place. Miss Etta Nolan, Queen of the Carroll County Farm Bureau, who lived in this community, rode the float.

The farmers, with the help of the County Extension Service, turned to raising cattle, pulpwood, and broilers. Finally, farming became secondary as a source of income and the men and women took public jobs.

The Roy Parrish Cabinet Company opened in 1941. The sons of Mr. and Mrs. Parrish, Jimmy, Lawrence, and Ralph, grew up in the business and remained when becoming adults.

In 1952, the Parrish Cabinet company building burned. The men in the community helped rebuild the shop by cutting logs, hauling them to the sawmill, and constructing the plant. When the building was finished, the Parrishes gave a barbecue to express their appreciation to those who participated in the "houseraising." In 1973, the Parrishes opened a retail furniture and appliance store.

The Center Point Fire Department was organized in 1975 when a fire truck was purchased. The Department was staffed with volunteers.

R.W. West was the road overseer in the community when all the roads were dirt. When a boy became sixteen, he was subject to a road tax of $3.00 per year. He could work on the roads at 50 cents per day until he paid the amount. The road machines were mule-drawn. At laying by time, the mules were used to pull the road machines. There were no paved county roads until after the 1930s and none in this area until the 1950s.

Mrs. Iva P. Levans provided information for the section above.

Draketown. Located eight miles north of Temple, Draketown was settled several years prior to the Civil War and was known as Long Leaf Post Office because of a tall, long leaf pine that grew nearby. The quiet little village came alive when copper was discovered and a band of miners arrived from Ducktown, Tennessee. An early settler, Elisha Brooks, remarked at the time that the drake of Georgia would beat the duck of Tennessee, meaning that more copper would be mined there than in Ducktown. For many years, the Tallapoosa Mines, as they were called, were very productive. Dr. R.B. Hutcheson practiced medicine in Draketown before and after the Civil War. In 1878, he was joined by Dr. W.F. Goldin. Doctors who practiced there later were B.F. Eaves, W.L. Hogue, and R.B. Goldin. In 1884, Draketown had dry goods stores, one barroom, a blacksmith shop, Masonic lodge, and a Baptist church. In 1906, the Draketown Baptist Institute opened in a new two-story building. By 1907, the Draketown Banking Company was serving the area. Today, Draketown is quiet little village with most of its residents working in businesses and industries of nearby towns.

Community Schools. In what is now the Temple School attendance area there were nine rural schools in 1918. The school year was six months. The schools were: Pine Grove, Oak Grove, Center Point, Harmony Grove, Bold Springs, Bethel, Mount Carmel, Taylor's, and Brooklyn.
Pine Grove. The new Pine Grove School on land lot 243, school district 30, south of Center Point was under construction. It had two classrooms, cloak rooms, and a teacher's office. It was planned by R.E. Lee, Rural School Architect, of South Carolina. There were two teachers and nine grades. The average pupil attendance was sixty-four. This building replaced a previous building which burned. The new building was remodeled later and became the home of the Jack Newsomes and is still occupied as a residence (Mote Rd at Center Point Rd).
Oak Grove was on lot 52, school district 36, two miles from Center Point. Grades one through seven were taught there by one teacher. It was a one-room school with an average attendance of thirty-six. The desks were homemade.

Center Point School had double patent desks. It was located on land lot 80, school district 36. One teacher taught seven grades. The average attendance was thirty-one.

Harmony Grove, one and one-half miles north of Center Point was located on land lot 110, school district 36. Students completed seven grades there. The average attendance was twenty-five. The desks were homemade.

Bold Springs School was located at Armstrong Road and Pleasant Ridge Church Road on land lot 318, school district 37. The children sat at homemade desks. One teacher taught seven grades. Thirty-five was the average attendance.

In the 1990s, former students and other interested parties began a drive to save the old Bold Springs school building. Due to their efforts, this historic structure was restored and moved to the Ag Center in Carrollton. A reunion of former students was held at the restored school whereby they each wrote their names on the blackboard, which was subsequently preserved.

Mount Carmel was north of Temple on land lot 267, school district 43. The average attendance was forty-nine. The pupils sat on long benches. They could complete the seventh grade there.

Taylor's was located one and one-half miles from Mt. Carmel on lot 265, school district 43. There were homemade desks and benches for the children. The teacher did not have a desk. Eight grades with an average attendance of thirty-four were taught by one teacher.

Brooklyn was two miles from Taylor's and two miles from Mt. Carmel. The building had two classrooms with homemade desks. The single teacher was responsible for teaching grades one through seven. An average attendance of twenty-six was maintained in 1918. Brooklyn was on land lot 201, school district 42. It replaced the old Brooks School.

Hickory Level School was also nearby on lot 56 in school district 35. It was three miles from Oak Grove. This was a two-room building. The children sat at homemade desks. The two teachers taught eight grades. Hickory Level averaged sixty-seven children. The school later consolidated with Villa Rica.

Lovell's School replaced *Bethel* and *Harmony Grove* in 1920. It was a two-teacher school. In 1928, Mrs. Myrtis Henry and Mae Baskin taught there. They enrolled thirty-seven pupils. Miss Ruth Wood was the principal and Mrs. H.B. Baskin was a teacher at Lovell's in 1933.

In 1928, eight rural schools were in operation in the present Temple school attendance area. Center Point consolidated with Temple in 1929. It was followed by Bold Springs, 1931; Brooklyn, 1934; Lovell's, 1938; Mt. Carmel and Oak Grove, 1939; Taylor's (Fairview), 1941; and Pine Grove in 1945.

Pine Grove School, 1918

Oak Grove School, 1918

Center Point School, 1918

Harmony Grove School, 1918

Bold Springs School, 1918

Mt. Carmel School, 1918

Taylor's School, 1918

Brooklyn School, 1918

Hickory Level School, 1918

(New) Bethel School, 1918

CHAPTER XVIII

TRAIN WRECKS

There was a train wreck at the trestle about one and one-half miles from downtown Temple in **1890**. It involved the collision of a westbound freight train and a work train. The engineer of the westbound train did not heed the warning of the flagman. The two engines met on the trestle throwing some of the cars off. The engineer of the westbound was killed and three others were injured.

Around **1907** or **1908**, a freight train stopped at the depot. There were a number of men, a lady, and her two children riding in the caboose. The men got off the train, but the lady, who was the wife of the telegraph operator at Villa Rica, and her two children remained. A freight train crashed into the caboose. The mother was killed and the children were injured.

In **1928**, a fast freight train wrecked at the depot. One car crashed into the side of the waiting room while another bumped into the side of the operator's office. Fortunately, no one was injured.

In **1950**, a 19 car pileup occurred along the curve in the tracks west of town. A rail car carrying benzene caught fire which resulted in the burning of additional cars as well. Both the Villa Rica and Douglasville fire trucks arrived on the scene but could not reach the wreckage. The Temple volunteer fire department did, however, manage to reach the blaze by driving their truck along a narrow path and then along the railroad right-of-way. They managed to extinguish the blaze completely thus saving numerous cars from burning. The Southern Railway superintendent on the scene praised the Temple fire fighters for their heroic efforts. Reportedly, several thousand people were witness to the wreckage. The cause of the accident was determined to be a broken wheel flange, the flange being the part of the wheel designed to create a snug fit to the rail. There were no injuries.

Thirty-two cars on an eastbound freight train derailed in Temple in July **1954**, making this the largest train wreck in Temple history. The accident resulted in an estimated one million dollars in damages. Many cars were tossed into the streets running from the depot to a considerable distance westward. A defective bearing box was believed to be the cause. Fortunately, there were no injuries.

In August **1966**, another freight train derailed at about the same location. This was also another exceedingly large wreck at 25 cars and resulted in an enormous dollar amount of damages. One of the boxcars landed on Sage Street only thirty yards from a residence. The cause of this accident was a defective wheel flange. Fortunately, there were no injuries.

In **1972**, a set of wheels on one of three rail cars carrying an enormous metal beam jumped the tracks. The metal beam purportedly weighed an estimated 250,000 pounds whereas each rail car carrying it weighed only about 100,000 pounds each. Local news reporters determined the beam was destined for a Cartersville location but failed to ascertain its purpose. A huge crane was used to set the beam and rail car back on the tracks. There were no injuries.

CHAPTER XIX

PROGRESS

In the early 1900s, **telephone service** reached Temple. Zach Adams and one helper installed the telephone system and set up the telephone exchange, which for a long time was called "Central Office." It was housed in the building next to the pharmacy. L.K. Smith representing the Gainesboro Company built the lines from Villa Rica to Temple. The Gainesboro Company sold out to Southern Bell in 1930. In small towns like Temple, callers typically knew the operators personally and often times would chat with the operator awhile before their call was connected. Some of the telephone operators were Mrs. Hallie Dewberry, Mrs. Pearl Dewberry, Miss Ruth Crawford, Miss Ruby Crawford, and Mrs. Anna Dodson. In 1930 there were 29 telephones in Temple each costing $2 per month.

Georgia Power Company served its first customers in Temple in April 1927.

Though the process of improving the main east-west road to better accommodate vehicles began well over a decade earlier, what was to become the **Bankhead Hwy (Hwy 78)** was not paved in this area until 1933. The highway was routed around downtown Temple so vehicles would not have to cross the railroad tracks.

On May 5, 1935, Temple voters approved a bond issue of $12,000. This, along with a $26,000 grant from the Works Progress Administration, financed the building of the **water system**. Dr. C.R. Hart was mayor. Council members were D.C. Williams, J.D. Askew, H.L. Cartwright, T.W. Ferguson, and R.T. Williams. At the completion of the system in 1936, H.L. Cartwright was chosen as the first superintendent. The water source was Webster Creek, named for an early settler. The pumping station was built beside the creek and the water tank was erected on Montgomery Street, across from the home of Mr. and Mrs. Frank Lambert. In 1954, an additional tank was built beside the Sewell Manufacturing Company on W. Johnson Street.

The first **R.E.A.** power lines reached customers in Carroll County in 1937. Roy and Hugh Richards constructed the lines.

W.C. Prichard built a **motel** soon after the close of World War II about two miles east of downtown Temple on Hwy 78. What later became known as Alden Motel was originally named Aluminum Court because, quite remarkably, each unit had an aluminum exterior. On April 12, 1952, Prichard sold to Ernest A. Ortenburg. He remodeled the structures and changed the name to Alden Motel, for his middle name. Colorful neon lights attached to each and every roof line lit up the night sky. Reba Smith Ortenburg operated the motel for several years. A restaurant/gift shop adjacent to the motel was added. Among other operators, the restaurant was purchased by Nolan and Barbara Cheek who operated it for more than 33 years until September 2001 when it was partially destroyed by fire. The motel marks a turning point as this business was borne of automobile transportation rather than the railway system.

**Early version of Alden Court with aluminum exterior;
hence the name Aluminum Court. Note each unit features a garage.
Built in the years following WWII.**

**Alden Courts Gift Shop, Circa 1954
Until the 1960s, the motel lit up the night with orange and green neon lighting.
A large assortment of yard ornaments includes pink flamingos.**

Temple bought its **first fire truck** in 1947 and F.L. Young was the first fire chief. Prior to that time, the water hoses were pulled to fires on a two-wheel cart hitched to a car.

Hwy 113 was blacktopped in 1951. Most streets in town were blacktopped in 1953 when C.A. Truitt was mayor.

A twenty-three acre lake, constructed in 1960, provided the town with water. In 1965, the Little Tallapoosa **Watershed** Lake of 308 acres was constructed southeast of Temple. It is locally called Lake Buckhorn, a name which was derived from the old Buckhorn Tavern.

Temple installed a **natural gas** system in 1962. The city sold its gas system to Atlanta Gas Light Company in 1978.

The **first traffic light** was installed in 1972 at the intersection of Highways 113 and 78. There are a total of six traffic lights now.

The Explorers, under the leadership of Richard Bracknell, assisted David Stephens fulfill his Eagle award project by installing the town's **first street signs** in 1976.

On December 22, 1977, **Interstate Highway 20** was opened through Temple.

The county, under the direction of Commissioner Horrie Duncan, built a modern county-city **fire station** at the intersection of East Sage Street and Highway 78 in 1980. The two-bay station serves a five-mile radius.

Cable TV service reached Temple in 1981 when West Georgia Cable installed lines in this area.

For reference on additional and more recent occurrences, please see Temple Today (2012).

CHAPTER XX

CLAIMS TO FAME

Casper Lassetter, the first graduate of Temple Model School, was the editor of the Mississippi-Arkansas-Louisiana and Kentucky-Tennessee-West Virginia Editions of the *Progressive Farmer* Magazine.

Ruth and Ruby Crawford, twin daughters of Mr. and Mrs. Hamp Crawford, achieved national prominence in the fields of banking, accounting, and law. Ruth served as a Georgia delegate to the Democratic National Convention in 1976.

Adrian Drew, valedictorian of Temple High School in 1939, flew an Air Force F101A setting a new world flight speed record in 1957. He was awarded the Thompson Trophy for this achievement. Temple honored him with a parade and barbecue.

Dr. Guy Wells was president of South Georgia Teachers College and Georgia State College for Women. He also organized the State School Superintendents Association and was president of the Georgia Education Association.

S.M. Cown, a teacher at Brooklyn School and husband of Mattie Brooks Cown, became the first county extension agent in Georgia and second in the nation when he accepted the position of Carroll County Farm Agent in 1907.

Isaac E. Cobb, longtime proprietor of Buckhorn Tavern, served in the State Legislature in the 1830s and 1840s.

Charles Thomas, Jr., a Temple attorney, was elected to the Georgia House of Representatives in 1978 from the 69th District.

Temple Mayor Hampton H. Sewell became a well-known evangelistic singer throughout the South in the early 1900s. He composed more than 500 songs and published four songbooks. His best known composition, "He Included Me," is an old standard in hymnals today.

The Temple Model School was founded by Villa Rica area resident Ira W. Williams. He is credited with conceiving the school's most innovative programs.

The first school transportation system in the state began at the Temple Model School. John F. Brooks led in the development of the system while under the leadership of school superintendent Ira W. Williams. Though the system employed mule and horse-drawn wagons, this was metaphorically speaking the state's first school bus program.

Paul Cobb was Regional Director of the Internal Revenue Service for many years.

In 1929, Carroll County led the state for the third consecutive year in cotton production. In 1936, the county led the state in number of farms with 4,699. Also in 1936, Carroll ranked second in the number of mules.

The Temple area especially held a reputation for growing large quantities of high quality cotton.

The Georgia High School Association began in Temple in 1905. It was organized by Temple Model School teacher Laura Josephine Rozar and UGA affiliated school inspector Dr. Joseph Stewart as the Northwest Georgia Association. The Association was later expanded and transformed into the statewide governing body of today.

The Temple Methodist Church is the oldest brick church building in the county.

J. Phil Campbell, Sr., a Temple native and Model School Teacher, served as Georgia Agriculture Commissioner.

Robert McBrayer, a Temple High School and Georgia Tech graduate, was an engineer and manager with NASA in a career spanning 38 years beginning in 1963 at the Johnson Manned Spacecraft Center in Houston before retiring as Director, Systems Management Office in 2001 at the Marshall Space Flight Center in Huntsville, AL. He made significant contributions to the Mercury, Gemini, Apollo, Skylab and Space Shuttle programs developing projects for flight survival, safety, payload, and experimentation. His awards include Directors Commendation Awards and NASA Exceptional Achievement Medals.

CHAPTER XXI

FACTS AND FOLKS

Many citizens remember the "Brush" as being the first car they saw.

John Rowe was the village shoemaker for many years. He charged twenty-five cents for repairing shoe soles.

The cotton seed oil mill operated twenty-four hours a day.

According to local lore, a Creek Indian Princess named Anne Crowlane is buried in Asbury Cemetery.

Charlie and Leon Lee operated a "rolling store."

Dan Whisenant was the village fiddler many years ago. He gave one-man concerts on the street and played for square dances.

John M. Baker made a trip to Europe in 1913. When he returned he published a booklet entitled *A Sketch of a Trip to Europe Made by J.M. Baker of Temple, Ga.* Mr. Baker had a fertilizer manufacturing plant in town in the early 1900s.

Mrs. Iva Spence Hendrix of Hog Liver Rd owned a leak proof wooden bathtub made by her father using poplar boards in 1896.

Young people often had picnics and wiener roasts at Webster Creek near the site of the old waterworks on Montgomery St. Baptisms were also held there.

Cecil Spence's school bus in 1929 had a wooden body.

Mrs. U.A. "Granny" Yearty (1883-1978) was born in Temple in the same year the city was chartered and continued to live here her entire life. She attended the early wooden school and wrote school assignments on a slate.

W.L. Steadham, Sr. had a Delco Plant which supplied electricity to his three stores and also to two churches.

J.M. Rutledge served as chief of police for thirty-five years from the 1940s until his retirement in 1982. As late as the1960s, he was the only police officer. He worked the night shift. There was no police on duty during the day.

Hamp Crawford operated a "jitney" (taxi) service in a Model-T Ford for the drummers who came to town. He also sold homemade ice cream and milkshakes which he "shook" himself.

Dr. C.R. Hart ran a drugstore in town for forty years.

There were two section houses between town and G.F. Moore's house. Railroad men lived in them.

In 1888, the Carroll Nursery of Temple was offering apple trees for ten cents each. Allen and Spake had a good supply of them on all first Tuesdays in Carrollton. This was the traditional trading day at the county seat.

Travelers commonly known as gypsies camped annually in J.W. Hill's woods at Hwy 113 and Rainey Road. The men traded mules and horses with Temple area residents. The ladies sold beautiful handmade lace for five cents a yard or exchanged it for butter, eggs, etc.

Many people reminisce about pound suppers, candy pullings, and serenading.

The historic wooden railroad crossing bridge at Croft Street in Carrollton received a $200,000 renovation recently. Farlan Floyd, a Temple resident, was the engineer for the renovation. The bridge was dedicated to his memory and a plaque was installed on the site at a ceremony on March 10, 2011.

Temple had a number of much needed public wells in front of the downtown stores to serve thirsty travelers and their horses.

Nettie Riggs was a substitute mail carrier for her father and the route took almost all day with the horse and buggy.

The mail sacks were brought from the depot to the post office in a two-wheel cart.

Many people remember John Michael as being one of the best singers they knew.

Public transportation was available throughout much of Temple's history. Passengers boarded the trains from the depot. Greyhound buses picked up passengers in front of the drugstore. Many local citizens traveled to work every day by train or bus. Others went on shopping excursions to the downtown Atlanta Rich's and other stores. Public transportation ended in Temple in the 1960s; soon after the depot was demolished.

"Dolph McBeth," an African-American man, was the only barber in town for many years. Haircuts were ten and fifteen cents.

Zach Adams owned the first automobile in town, a one-cylinder Brush.

In the 1940s, the Major Temple Garden Club planted 1800 pink running rose bushes along the Highway 78 corridor. Tourists often stopped to take pictures or get cuttings.

It was not unusual to get a cinder in your eye when the coal-burning locomotives went through town.

On June 1, 1984, a runner carrying the Olympic Torch traversed the Hwy 78 corridor through Temple en route to the 1984 Summer Olympics held in Los Angeles.

A train called the Accommodation carried passengers to and from Atlanta. It was so named because it made frequent stops.

For many years, the fire siren was sounded every Saturday at noon.

Claude Morris kept stobs in front of his café for the men in town to play horseshoes. Mr. Morris was in business for over 50 years.

S.W. Roberts, Sr. trapped quail and sold them to Pete Lewis for ten cents each in the early 1900s. They were served at the hotel.

Roy Brazeal served as principal of Temple School longer than any other – fourteen years.

In 1888, lightning hit the V.R. Davis house and knocked two legs off a table and two holes in the syrup barrel. About three gallons ran out on the floor before it was discovered.

In 1929, the Temple P.T.A. had a "hen drive" to make money for some new desks. Each child was to bring a hen or the price of one.

Temple received a second charter November 23, 1901. The population of Temple was 397 in 1900.

Bold Springs School was the site of the court ground for the Kansas district in 1913.

Temple native Knox Walker, Sr. served as president of the Georgia Education Association and also served as interim superintendent of Fulton County schools.

V.R. Davis of Temple patented a car-coupler in 1888.

The Atlanta Journal-Constitution published thirty-five *Georgia Dateline* articles about the Temple area in 1977-78. Most of the articles are of a historical nature and are fascinating human interest stories as well.

In 1933, mothers of the P.T.A. sold homemade ice cream from a booth in town on Saturdays to buy textbooks for children whose parents could not afford them.

In 1941, sixteen of the thirty-seven county school buses had wooden bodies.

Dr. Lucius E. Kinney began his practice of dentistry in 1925. He is the only dentist that has ever practiced here. In the 1930s he moved his practice to Villa Rica.

There are at least five other Temples in the United States. They are in the states of Texas, New Hampshire, Maine, Oklahoma, and Louisiana. Temple, Texas was named for Bernard M. Temple, chief engineer of the Santa Fe Railroad built through that city. He was the brother of Robert H. Temple, for whom our town of Temple, GA was named. Temple, New Hampshire was named in

1768 for the Provincial Lieutenant Governor, Sir John Temple. The first settlers of Temple, Maine were from New Hampshire. They named their new town for Temple, New Hampshire. Temple, Oklahoma was named for Temple Houston, a son of Sam Houston. Temple, Louisiana was named for its first postmaster, Edgar Temple.

The northern boundary of the Carroll County panhandle, less than 4 miles north of Temple, coincides with the boundary which divided the Creek and Cherokee nations.

The Henry Cartwrights were in business for 47 years. Mrs. Cartwright was well known for the delicious fried pies that she made and sold.

In 1976, Peggy Dunaway was elected as the first woman to serve on the city council.

Roy Baxter received a new 1926 Chevrolet coupe from his parents when he graduated from high school. It became a fixture in the garage of their Sage St home where it was quite visibly parked for the next six decades. The Baxter family has it still.

The graduating class of 1914 consisted of four young ladies.

Dr. S.F. Scales opened a hospital on the second floor of the Hickory Level Store in 1927. It consisted of an operating room, two wards, nurse's room, consultation room, office, waiting room, running water and lights.

The Senior Class of 1936 was the first to wear caps and gowns at Temple High. The Class of 1937 was the first to take a trip to Washington, D.C.

Dr. T. M. Spruell organized the Ford owners of the county in 1913. The social organization met each spring at the Kingsberry Bridge on the Little Tallapoosa River in Carrollton.

The Temple Academy had an enrollment of 40 in 1885. By 1891, there were 114 pupils, the fifth largest school in the county. The public school term was five months.

Bill Benson of Carrollton met the Temple trains in 1885. His hack line carried passengers to and from Carrollton for $1.00 each way. A one-way trip took three hours.

In 1946, the Hill family opened the Temple Theater on W. Johnson Street. The first movie starred Deanna Durbin. Bill Green was a projectionist at the theatre.

The 1913 Curfew Law stated the residents under the age of eighteen must be off the streets by 8 p.m. during the winter months and by 9 during the summer unless accompanied by a parent or guardian or could show sufficient reason for being on the streets. A first offense called for a reprimand and second offense resulted in a fine not to exceed $2 or a stay in the calaboose not to exceed one day.

The street tax in 1914 was $3.50 per year or seven days' work.

In 1921, the town voted to make the James Street Railroad Crossing the center of the town as per the amended charter. Previously, the depot was the center.

The speed limit for automobiles and motorcycles was ten miles per hour in 1911. An auto was to stop immediately if the driver of a horse or mule-drawn vehicle warned that the automobile was frightening the animal.

Among the Temple Mayors have been: Jesse Kinney, H.H. Sewell, Rufus Williams, W.B. Chandler, J.E. Edmondson, J.N. Hildebrand, Clarence E. Ringer, C.L. Baskin, J.T. Brown, C.R. Hart, L.T. Stevens, J.T. West, W.B. Manley, F.L. Young, W.L. Adcock, C.A. Truitt, Herman Riggs, Homer McColister, Bill Steadham, I.J. Holder, Olin Johnson, L.L. Rainey, Homer Williams, Jeff Hansard, Harry Shadrix, Lester Harmon, and Rick Ford.

W.L. Adcock was president of the Carroll County Board of Education from 1948 to 1951.

One hundred red, white, and blue, helium-filled balloons were released at the 100th birthday party for the post office on April 24, 1982. Citizens of the following towns found balloons and responded to the attached messages: Duluth, Hull, Carlton, Dacula, Marietta, Powder Springs, and Roswell, Georgia. One traveled to Abbeville, S.C.

John F. Brooks became Superintendent of Carroll County Schools in 1929.

A canning plant was constructed on the school campus in the fall of 1935.

During the pioneer days, gold was mined on a farm south of Temple owned by William N. Davis.

James (Jimmy) Watson, Jr., a Temple rural mail carrier, is a relative of Thomas E. Watson, the US Senator who in 1893 pushed the bill through Congress originating Rural Free Delivery. The James F. Watson, Sr. family planted crepe myrtles in front of the current Post Office in honor of the Watson family and the Temple postal heritage.

The first Temple correspondent to the Carroll Free Press was E.L. Connell.

The proper name for Williams Mill Creek, south of Temple, is Savanachee according to an 1890 issue of the Carroll Free Press.

A favorite picnic spot for Temple young people in the 1890s was Baskin's double bridges, located between Hwy 113 and Hickory Level Store.

Walker's Hotel was the commercial travelers' headquarters in Carroll County and the scene of many social gatherings of the elite.

In the Brooklyn Community, Taylor's Congregational Methodist Church and nearby Taylor's (Fairview) School burned on the same night in February 1929.

One of the most iconic, nationally recognized Civil War photographs is a portrait of Stephen Pollard (1830-1899) who lived nearby in Haralson County and is buried at Liberty Christian

Church Cemetery. The photograph is seen in numerous history books and in the acclaimed Ken Burns PBS documentary of the Civil War.

Livestock freely roamed the countryside until the Temple district passed the fence law on March 7, 1887.

The first Tuesday of each month was an important day in Carrollton. Farmers congregated on the First Tuesdays for a day of visiting and transacting business. Trading was usually brisk at the mule yard.

The original 1882 plat of Temple lots includes the names of streets. They are Level, Bell, Camp, Griffin, Rowe, Sawmill, Clark, Riggs, Sage, Jackson, Brooks, Montgomery, James, Carrollton, Johnson, Tallapoosa, and Buchanan. Most of the names were apparently in honor of early residents and railroad employees.

During World War II, all five Holder brothers, Floyd, Hoyt, J.M., Lamar and Burell served in the Armed Forces at the same time.

The fire station, in 1982, the town's Centennial year, was manned by Bill Benton, Fire Chief, and firemen Kenny Eskew and Royce Henry. Volunteer Firemen were Johnny Hopson, Burt Stevens, Bobby Pope, Gerald Henry, Keith Lewis, Bill Cash, Robert Gordon, Mark Haney, Harry Shadrix, L.E. Carroll, Ray Pope, Danny Carden, Carl Maples, Anthony Eskew, Doyce Henry, Ronald Fortner, Tony Davidson, and Chuck Dempsey. Kurt Eulenfeld was Chief of Police.

Allen Stevens gave several acres of land for the building site of Sewell Manufacturing Company. Citizens of the town raised $8,000 to pave the plant's parking lot.

The population of Temple in 1982 was 1,520.

J.M. Huey helped survey the town lots in 1882.

Frontier era settlers were known to, on occasion, hurl insults by accusing one another of being Pony Club members. In at least one instance, a lawsuit was filed for slander.

After the Pony Club was driven from Carroll County, the group continued their thieving ways in Paulding County where they were driven out two years later. Some members were allowed to remain, however. The town of Yorkville is named after former Pony Club member Josiah York.

In the decades after the Pony Club was banished from the area, this infamous group became the source of a number of novels and short stories. Word of the Pony Club even traveled overseas. A fictional work, *The Pony Club: A Tale of the Backwoods Settlements of Georgia* by Richard Bentley, was published in London in 1846 in "Bentley's Miscellany", a publication at one time edited by Charles Dickens. William Gilmore Simms, a popular Southern historian and novelist, whose works received high praise from Edgar Allen Poe, wrote a number of novels incorporating the exploits of the Pony Club as well.

Longtime Temple High School coach Donald Stitcher received a tryout with the Atlanta Crackers.

Gerald Carroll signed a minor league baseball contract with the Milwaukee Braves in 1960. Carroll was brought to the attention of scouts by major league baseball pitching great and Haralson County resident Whitlow Wyatt.

Media mogul and former Atlanta Braves owner Ted Turner was known to visit Thomas Hardware (corner of Carrollton and Tallapoosa Streets) to purchase fishing tackle en route to fishing outings with his friend, Whitlow Wyatt, at Wyatt's lake nearby in Haralson County. Turner purchased a portion of Wyatt's property.

Barry Lewis coached the Temple 16-Under Hotshots to a national USSSA slow-pitch softball title in 1998.

Longtime mayor Harry Shadrix batted .525 in 1961 for the Carrollton Lakers, a semi-pro baseball team.

Harry Shadrix was inducted into the National Fast Pitch Softball Hall of Fame in 2011.

The Temple High School girls' basketball team won the State Championship in 1978.

Donna Conaway Johnson, a member of the 1978 State championship basketball team and later a coach at Temple High School, scored a combined total of 2249 points in high school and collegiate games. She was named The Atlanta Journal- Constitution Player of the Year and also set a State record in the Discus Throw both in 1978.

Ruth and Ruby Crawford stumped the panel on the Television program *What's My Line?* as identical twin lawyers in 1954, a time when their profession was a rarity for women. The Crawford twins appeared on *Oprah* in 2000. Their dog was "interviewed" on the national NBC evening news in 1977 at the Inauguration of President Jimmy Carter, for whom the Crawford twins made numerous campaign appearances. The twins were invited to a number of events at the White House during the Carter presidency.

The Historic Preservation Division of the Georgia DNR named the Levans farm a Centennial Family Farm in 2009, meeting the requirement of 100 years of ownership by a single family. This Center Point farm has remained in the Levans family for seven generations.

Joseph R. McCain published a book, *Christian Dispensation and the Restoration of Israel*, in 1885. Two copies are housed at the Harvard University divinity school library.

Joseph L. Saul, a Lithuanian immigrant, owned and operated a clothing store on Sage Street from 1917 to 1925. Descendants of Mr. Saul continued the family retailing tradition founding Atlanta area retailers Saul's Department Stores, Turtles Records, and Chapter 11 Books.

Betty J. Stevens owns over 5000 cookbooks. She appeared on the *Rachael Ray* show in 2008 to discuss her hobby.

Tara Hatfield of "Tara's Tiny's Farm," located at 62 Oak Grove Road, breeds and sells Nubian and Nigerian Dwarf goats. Pet goat milk and goat milk soap are for sale, also.

An interesting trivia question was aired on CBS Atlanta News on July 18, 2011. The question was, "In what city is the shortest landlocked highway in the state?" The answer is Temple. East Sage and James Streets comprise State Route 274. It is sometimes referred to as "The Loop."

Some few remaining Temple residents can recall seeing the "Best Friend of Charleston" while on display in Temple for about an hour on August 9, 1929. Built in 1828, it is the first locomotive constructed for regular railroad service.

Jane McBrayer West operated a 5&10 cent store on Sage Street (second storefront from Carrollton Street) from 1943 until 1967.

In the 1950s, before many local residents owned a TV, Thomas Hardware (Sage Street at Carrollton Street) left one turned on in the display window after hours where groups gathered outside at night to watch ball games.

In 1951, Temple School purchased its first 16mm projector, an RCA Model 400, at a cost of $400.00. It was paid for by showing movies on Saturday night at the school auditorium and charging 10 cents admission.

When senior English teacher Mrs. Homer L. Turner asked for a volunteer to plow a Victory Garden for Temple High School during WWII, Lester Gray volunteered to do it. (Needless to say he got a good grade!) Other war time efforts included V-Mail, Ration Books, scrap metal drives and War Bonds.

The former Cown residence at 679 Cown Road was submitted for listing on the National Register of Historic Places. Approval could not yet be confirmed at press time.

CHAPTER XXII

ARCHITECTURE

Temple is a unique place in space and time. Though the town's historic development as a railroad community may share similarities with others, the land, people and events of Temple's history combined to create a distinct heritage. The heritage is richly reflected in the built environment surrounding us daily. Temple retains much of the historic character defined by the railroad corridor, nineteenth and twentieth century houses and stores, and other cultural landscape elements.

A Survey of Historic Resources conducted by the CFRDC Historic Preservation Planner identified approximately 110 historic properties. Temple's historic resources are primarily residential and commercial. Whereas most of the residences are on frame construction, most of the commercial buildings are of brick and rubble masonry.

The Survey determined the strongest concentration of historic resources is in the downtown commercial area and residences along Johnson and Carrollton (Hwy 113) Streets. This area may be eligible for listing in the National Register as a historic district.

Additionally, the Survey cited 10 structures as potentially eligible for inclusion in the National Register individually. This list includes Temple Methodist Church, the Temple Pharmacy building, five additional downtown store buildings, one house at Montgomery/Tallapoosa, one East Johnson Street house, and one Carrollton St. house.

The properties identified as individually significant and as a potential Historic District listed with the National Register are worthy of preservation, the study concluded.

This survey suggested Temple develop a historic resources preservation plan. Many of the historic buildings are in a state of deterioration. Much of our heritage is in danger of being lost.

Log Construction. Log construction was the earliest form of building in Carroll County. After the early settlers chose their homesites, they used the trees and fieldstones close at hand for their simple cabins. The settlers cut the trees and then hewed and weathered the logs.

The sills, or bottom logs, were often hardwoods since they were more resistant to rotting than pines. Sills were placed on a foundation of fieldstone piers. Walls were made of logs notched at the corners. Spacings between the logs were chinked with mud, wood, and stones in the winter, and in the summer the chinking was removed to allow light and air to enter.

Log structures were generally one room with a window cut out next to the chimney located at one end; a door was cut out of the front.

The Buckhorn Tavern, a double log house, was built in the 1830s. The two log rooms were separated by a breezeway which was often called a "dog trot" or "possum trot" because animals often sought shade in the summer here. The tavern was dismantled in 2001.

Plantation Plain, 1830-1840. Log construction was followed by a technique called heavy timber. This type of construction consisted of hand-hewn logs on a sill and corners with bracing, combined with small machine sawn pieces of wood. This technique allowed buildings to be 1½ or 2 stories tall. These plain, unadorned structures were typically oriented with their broad side toward the road, giving them a larger appearance. In this period of social consciousness, houses were usually close to the road rather than oriented among natural aspects.

It is not uncommon for homes to be constructed in a style more popular in a previous era. At times, home owners wish to live in the style of house in which they were raised. The following examples are of the Plantation Plain design, but are believed to be constructed later than the customary time period.

The Conaway house, located on the east side of Carrollton Street several parcels south of Hwy 78, is an example of this type of design. This 1½ story frame structure is one room deep with a front shed porch and several additions to the rear. The design of the windows indicates post-Civil War construction. This house is, nevertheless, one of the oldest in Temple.

Another example of plantation plain construction is the former Cown residence at 679 Cown Road built 1870-1874. It is currently the only house in the Temple area submitted for inclusion to the National Register of Historic Places. This is a 2-story structure with a front porch extending from both floors. The porch is supported by 13-inch square columns. The original builder, John Wesley Brooks, and his descendants figure most prominently in the history of the area. The house remained occupied by the family and contained most of the 1800s furnishings until the passing of Corinne Cown in 2008.

VICTORIAN STYLE, 1870-1900. The city of Temple developed after the Civil war, a time period most often referred to formally as Reconstruction. The architectural traditions reflect this pattern. There are few true examples of the Plantation Plain or Greek Revival styles in Temple, since these styles represent a previous time period. There are, however, homes built later which contain elements of these styles. Conversely, styles popular after the Civil War including **Victorian Vernacular**, **Victorian Gothic** and **Queen Anne** are well represented. In the 1880s, the South shifted from an almost completely agricultural economy to an agricultural-industrial economy. With the industrial revolution, there was a rise in the mobility of the middle class. Home construction was less costly, thanks to machines. During this period, people moved from rural areas into communities. They built houses close to each other, and near tree-lined streets with small front yards of swept dirt, defined by hedges and fences. Back yards were large and contained outbuildings and garden spaces.

A new construction technique called balloon framing consisted of machine sawn 2x4's with no large hand hewn members. Balloon framing and the use of smaller pieces of wood served to free house forms from the square, allowing rooms and porches to be any shape, with bay projections, gables, etc. The machine age is reflected in the decorative woodwork of the exterior of homes, sometimes referred to as gingerbread. Decorative shingles and spindles are other elements often seen in area homes which also reflect the Victorian love of ornamentation.

Victorian Vernacular, 1870-1880s. The M.E.V. Spence home place at Center Point is an outstanding example. This white, frame 1½ story home has a cat slide roof and a kitchen separated from the main 2-story portion. The house features a Victorian 2-story decorative portico with decorative sawn work. The setting makes this a picturesque example of a Southern farm home. Mrs. Pearl Raburn, daughter of Mr. Spence, lives in the home as of 1982.

Victorian Gothic, 1870-1880s. While previous architectural styles associated with the ideals of the Greeks and Romans, medieval forms became popular during this period. Many religious structures are of this style.

The First Baptist Church is a brick structure built in the Gothic style with towers of unequal height. Americans felt that uneven towers were a historically correct interpretation of the great

Gothic cathedrals, such as Chartres. The truth is, Chartres was constructed with towers of equal height; when a fire destroyed one tower, it was never rebuilt to match the original one.

The Temple Methodist Church, built in 1898, is the first brick church building constructed in Carroll County. The bricks were laid in common bond with one row of headers (end of brick) and five to seven rows of stretchers (long side of brick). This church building combines features of both the Gothic and Romanesque forms. The entranceway, with its rounded arches, refers to the Romanesque style, as does the pointed stained-glass windows and pointed towers.

The Warner A. Enterkin house built in 1880, (Montgomery at West Buchanan Street), with its three decorative gables, characterize it as Victorian Gothic. The Larry Mann home on the west side of Carrollton Street, two parcels south of Hwy 78, is also of this style.

Queen Anne Style, 1890s. The Queen Ann Style is the Victorian Period at its most decorative. These structures usually have a tower or turret, asymmetrical roof line, windows of all shapes and sizes, and a wrap-around porch, often with gazebos. Two examples in Temple are the Gladys Ivey home place on East Johnson Street and the J. M. Baxter home place at Carrollton Street and Hwy 78.

Pyramidal Style. Many simple, well-built homes are difficult to classify stylistically. One feature these one-story frame structures share is a high, pyramidal roof. The J.W. Hill home place on Asbury Road has a pyramidal roof.

Downtown Commercial. Temple's commercial district runs parallel to the railroad tracks. The one and two-story structures are made of brick as a fire precaution, as they share a common wall. Commercial buildings are divided into two zones. The parapet (or roof line) is usually decorative, with brick corbelling. Since the buildings have even setbacks, this ornamentation of the roof line identifies one building from another. The bottom zone, at the street level, usually features large-pane windows supported by cast iron columns. The doorway may be recessed.

Neo-Classical, 1900-1920. Around the turn of the century there was a reaction against the excessive ornamentation of the Victorian Period, and the Greek and Roman styles again became popular. These homes often contain features such as asymmetrical roof lines with addition of classical features, such as white columns, sidelights, and transoms over doors. The former G.M. Burns home fronting Tallapoosa Street at Montgomery Street is an example of this style.

Craftsman, 1900-1920. This style represents a new philosophy in architecture. It emphasizes simple, handcrafted uses of materials, in reaction against the machine-made ornamentation of the Victorian styles and the formality of the historical revival styles. The *Craftsman Bungalows* are one-story frame structures with a gable facing the road. They generally have a front porch supported by thick columns set on stone or brick piers. Another feature of the Craftsman style is the brackets supporting an overhanging roof. Windows are generally one clear pane in the bottom sash, while the upper sash will be divided into a decorative design. The former C.M. Morris home on Carrollton Street is of the Craftsman Bungalow style.

Post World War II Cottage. After World War II, a number of small cottages were constructed. Generally, these cottages are covered with shingles. For the first time, homes were built without the Southern front porch.

Ranch Style 1950-present. Ranch homes are one-story, sometimes split-level buildings, often of brick veneer. Generally, they approximate a Colonial, Spanish, or French style. These well-built homes typify American suburban development. They are often situated well back from the road with open, grassy lawns. The A.W. Hitchcock residence on Center Point Road is ranch style.

Information in this chapter was provided by Maurie Gail Golsen, Historic Preservation Planner, Chattahoochee-Flint Area Planning and Development Commission.

Plantation Plain, 268 Carrollton Street
One of the Oldest Houses in Temple

Plantation Plain, 679 Cown Road

Victorian Vernacular, 2490 Center Point Road

Victorian Gothic, 265 Carrollton Street

Queen Anne, 627 E. Johnson Street

Pyramidal, Asbury Road

Neo-Classical, 82 Tallapoosa Street

Craftsman Bungalow, 145 Carrollton Street

Ranch, 570 Center Point Road

CHAPTER XXIII

ROBERT HENRY TEMPLE

Robert Henry Temple, for whom the town of Temple is named, was Chief Engineer of the Georgia Pacific Railroad. He was a genuine "railroad man." The roads he built were considered among the best in the South. It is unlikely that this small town could have chosen a better man to honor.

His great-great-grandfather was Joseph Temple, a wealthy Englishman, who came to the Virginia Colony in 1722. He settled in Essex County. His five sons were all officers in the Revolution. They were Joseph, Liston, William, Samuel, and Benjamin, who was Robert's great-grandfather. By fighting against England they lost all their inheritance in the Temple English Estates.

His great-grandfather was Colonel Benjamin Temple of King William County, Virginia. He was a Lieutenant Colonel of the 4th Regiment of Continental Dragoons during the Revolutionary War. He became George Washington's right hand man.

Robert Temple's grandparents were Robert and Elizabeth Skyren Temple who settled in Ampthill Plantation, Chesterfield County, Virginia. Ampthill is now within the city limits of Richmond.

Robert Henry Temple was born September 25, 1831, at Oakley Plantation in Gloucester County, Virginia. He grew up at Berclair Plantation, seven miles southwest of Fredericksburg. He was the oldest son of Benjamin (1802-1872) and Lucy Lilly Robinson Temple (1807-1884). The family lived at Locust Grove Plantation in Middlesex County in the early 1830s. In 1839, they moved to Berclair Plantation in Spotsylvania County. They also had a town house in Fredericksburg. Benjamin and Lucy Lilly Temple were the parents of twelve children born between 1827 and 1849. They were: Elizabeth Lilly, Virginia Nelson, Robert Henry, Charles Wellford, Nollie Brooks, Judith Willantina, Benjamin Brooks, John Taylor, William Skyren, Bernard Moore, Ludwell Robinson, and Lucy Lilly. They were all reared at Berclair. Temple's father was the wealthiest man in Spotslvania County according to the 1860 U.S. Census. The Temples were Episcopalians.

In 1850, Temple was attending school and living at the home of his parents. As a young man, he moved to Richmond, Virginia. He married Lucy Ann Crouch. They had one son, John Twohig, born December 24, 1869. John Twohig married Nina R. Darvin. They had no children.

On April 18, 1862, Temple was appointed to serve in the Nitre and Mining Bureau of the Confederate War Department. He also served on the Railroad Commission. He was paroled from service on June 12, 1865, at Shreveport, Louisiana. As was the custom in the era after the war, Temple continued to be addressed by his rank; thus he was known as Major Temple.

Temple first entered railway service in 1852 as a rodman and leveler with the New Orleans, Jackson, and Great Northern Railroad. Between 1852 and 1881, he served as engineer or chief engineer for fifteen different railroad companies. From 1881 to February 1887, Temple became the Chief Engineer of the Georgia Pacific and constructed the railroad through Temple.

During the Civil War most of the railroads in the South were destroyed. Afterwards the job of reconstructing them and building new ones was at hand. Temple was a freelance engineer. He would survey a route, map it, and get the necessary information together. He would then try to interest investors in building the road and, in some instances, get the job of superintending the construction.

Temple put an end to friendships during the construction of a road and became severe taskmaster. He was so independent that he would never accept passes on the road he was building but always paid his fare when traveling.

Once a group of northern capitalists was invited to consider putting up the capital to build a proposed road. They came down and the project was talked over for days and days. Robert Temple had about given up hope of interesting the investors. One morning, after a long and tiresome session, he got up and told the group that had been given all the information he had and that he was through. He very emphatically stated that if they were going to build the road, build it. If not, he advised them to get on the train and go home. They built the road.

Robert Temple had two good-size cuts on the wall of his office. One pictured a man being carried out on a stretcher. The caption under it read, "This man was talked to death." The other showed a man seated at a table counting his money. The caption under this one read, "This man made a fortune attending to his own business." When a long-winded or inquisitive visitor wore out his welcome, Robert Temple would fix his gaze on the picture which applied. This always had the desired effect.

Bernard Moore Temple, a younger brother of Robert, was also an engineer specializing in railroad construction. He was Chief Engineer of the Santa Fe when it was built through Texas. Temple, Texas was named in honor of him when the railroad was built through the area in 1881. At that time, the area was amid a cotton growing section. The same was true of Temple, Georgia, in 1882. Berclair, Texas was named for the brothers' childhood home.

After a long career as an engineer specializing in railroad construction, Robert Henry Temple returned to his native soil, Virginia. The final resting place of Robert and Lucy Temple is the Hollywood Cemetery in Richmond. He died on December 22, 1901.

Rails of steel, which symbolize Robert Temple's dedicated years of service to the railroad industry, serve as a memorial to him. Robert Temple was strong – Robert Temple was a railroad man.

Courtesy, W.R. Dillard

Berclair Plantation, Childhood Home of Major Temple,
Near Fredericksburg, Virginia

CHAPTER XXIV

WE CELEBRATE

Temple has seen countless celebrations throughout its history starting with the celebration held in conjunction with the selling of town lots in 1882 as described in Chapter VII. Accounts of some of the more notable celebratory events occurring in the years that followed are included in this chapter.

Parade Entries. A replica of the Temple Methodist Church was presented on a float in the 1927 *Carroll County Centennial Parade*. Temple's float in the *Tournament of Books Parade* held in Carrollton in 1957 was a reproduction of a Temple Model School wagon. Temple's entry in the *US Bicentennial Parade* in 1976 held in the county seat again was a replica of a Model School wagon. This replica Model School wagon was fashioned by Johnny Muse and Harvey Holman.

Temple Model School. The city of Temple held a celebration in conjunction with the laying of a cornerstone for the Temple Model School on October 3rd, 1903. It was attended by a large crowd and included speeches and a dinner. The orator of the day was U.S. Congressman William Charles Adamson of Carrollton, for whom Adamson Square in Carrollton is named. Mayor Hamp Sewell and School Superintendent Ira W. Williams also gave speeches. The cornerstone was carved of a single piece of pristine white marble hand chiseled with the inscription "Laid by the Grand Lodge of Georgia, Oct. 3, 1903, A.D. 5903, Max Meyerhardt G.M." (Max Meyerhardt was Grand Master of the Georgia Masons at the time.) Included also in the inscription were the names of the mayor, city council, building committee, architect, and contractor.

The cornerstone was opened in the early 1950s after most of the building was destroyed by a fire. Items found in the cornerstone were: (1) a copy of the Oct. 3, 1903 edition of *The Atlanta Journal*; (2) a copy of the Sept. 9, 1903 edition of *Christian Observer*; (3) one section of the Sept. 29, 1903 edition of *The Atlanta News*; (4) a copy of the Oct. 1, 1903 edition of *Wesleyan Christian Advocate;* (5) a Southern Railway pass and a Central of Georgia Railway pass both issued to the editor of the *Banner Ledger*, published in Buchanan; (6) a note from Mayor Hamp Sewell; (7) two sheets bearing the letterhead of Temple doctor Charles L. Baskin one of which lists the members of the Temple Board of Education; (8) a note bearing the letterhead of the U.S. Post Office depicting an eagle presented by the Temple Postmaster; (9) a document with embossed emblem presented by the Independent Order of Odd Fellows Lodge No. 122 listing the officers and members; (10) a genealogy of the Griffin family; (11) a picture of 4-year-old Harold Walker Griffin with his puppy; (12) a bullet with an accompanying note which stated the bullet was found in 1864 at the site of a Civil War battle near Dallas, Georgia; (13) a Bible; (14) some coins, 6 pennies, 7 nickels, 3 dimes; (15) a business envelope with the inscription Griffin Bros., Dealers in General Mdse. which contained a sheet listing the members of the Griffin family; (16) a receipt for a Money Order from the Temple Post Office dated Oct. 5, 1903; (17) the (Methodist) *Senior Quarterly* 1903; (18) the (Baptist) *Intermediate Quarterly* 1903, [priced at 2 cents per quarter]; and (19) an ink blotter with advertising which read Chickamauga Buggy Co., Wholesale Buggy Builders, Chattanooga.

Sewell Manufacturing. Another ceremony for the creation of a time capsule was held on July 13, 1953 at the 27,000 square foot Sewell Manufacturing Company building at 261 West Johnson St. The cornerstone actually consisted of two separate marble slabs set within the bricks near the corner of the building. The two slabs were chiseled with the words "For God and Country" and "In

Appreciation of the City of Temple, 1953," respectively. The items placed within included: (1) a Handbook for fall and winter 1953-54, showing models and a picture of executives and sales representatives; (2) a panorama picture of city leaders and Sewell workers; (3) a list of officers and directors; (4) a card showing a picture of the Bremen Sewell building;(5) a balance sheet for the city of Temple as of May 31, 1953; and (6) several coins.

The Sewell building and surrounding 8 acres were purchased by the city in 2007. Plans were made to demolish the building and construct a new city hall on the site. The cornerstone was opened in a ceremony on January 23, 2013. In attendance were relatives of former city officials from the time the plant was built along with former employees of the plant. The contents were removed by Mayor Rick Ford. Unfortunately, the contents retrieved were damaged by moisture and so were in poor condition. The building was demolished soon thereafter. The mayor stated his desire to install a new cornerstone within the walls of the new city hall when constructed.

Temple Centennial. The Temple Centennial Committee was approved by the mayor and council in January 1982 for the purpose of planning a Centennial Celebration. Members of the committee were B.W. Holder, Chairman; Claudia Waldrop, Vice Chairman; Johnny Muse, Secretary; and Steve Cash, Treasurer. Other members were Gail Conaway, Richard Bracknell, Dorothy Burton, Nolan Cheek, Sammy Hathcock, Darnell Powell, Gary Parrish, Melba Karr, Barbara Senft, Ruth Holder, Mark Haney, Larry Boswell, Harry Shadrix, Bobby Gentry, Caroline B. Hudsputh, Jane Pope, and Charles Thomas, Jr.

A full week of festivities was planned starting September 25th beginning with a community worship service then featuring various evening entertainment throughout the week. Other activities included a Miss Centennial Pageant, arts and crafts fair, beard growing contest, and a street dance.

Founders' Day. Since 2009 the city holds a Founders' Day celebration in September. It typically features entertainment, arts and craft fair, a history display, and a host of other activities.

Road Banner over Sage Street for the Town's Centennial

CHAPTER XXV

TEMPLE 2013

The City of Temple has seen many changes since *A History of Temple, Georgia,* was published in 1982. It has experienced tremendous growth in population and housing. Temple's proximity to Atlanta and Interstate 20 has made it one of the fastest growing cities in Carroll County. However, the recent downturn in the economy has slowed the growth. Some are without jobs, and some are facing foreclosure on their homes.

The 2010 U.S. Census statistics, which were released March 17, 2011, show that Temple's population almost doubled in the past decade. Temple grew from 2,383 residents living within the city limits in 2000 to 4,228 in the latest statistics.

The City Hall, presently located at 337 Sage Street, continues to provide leadership and services to the city. Rick Ford is the mayor, and council members are Terron Bivins, Larry Mann, Hiley Miller, William Simmons, and Richard Bracknell. Angie Costner is the City Clerk, and Kim Pope is the City Administrator.

Many new subdivisions have been built in the Temple area during the past few years. An interesting note is that two of the subdivisions used historic themes. Stagecoach Subdivision was built in the area where the once famous Buckhorn Tavern stood. When the tavern was torn down in 2001, Gene Merritt retrieved and numbered each log allowing for potential reconstruction. In 2002, before developer David Harrison built the subdivision, historian Doug Mabry headed an archaeological dig which turned up more than 1,000 artifacts including horseshoes, railroad spikes, chinaware fragments, animal bones, buckles and various other objects. Also, SchoolHouse Trace Townhomes, located at the corner of James and Griffin Streets, were built on the site of the once famous Model School. The marble cornerstone and 50,000 bricks (which were cleaned by hand) were used in the construction. The house numbers even start with 1904, which was the opening date of the Model School. Brad Parks was the developer.

Two travel centers were built near Interstate 20. MAPCO Express Travel Center at 625 Carrollton Street just off I-20 at Exit 4 became Williams Express in 1999, and later became Pilot Travel Center. Flying J Travel Plaza, located at 650 Carrollton Street, opened in 1999. The two travel centers became Pilot Flying J on July 1, 2010.

Temple now has a Dollar General, Fred's, AutoZone and a Waffle House. Fast foods include Hardee's, Wendy's, McDonald's, and two Subway shops. Wendy's uses a historical theme as its decor. Hardee's originally used a historical theme but discontinued it when they remodeled. The pictures now hang in city hall. Mexican and Chinese foods are available as well as pizza, barbeque and country cooking. Little Tigers Learning Center was built at 150 West Perennial Drive. An 82,000- square foot Ingles Super Store opened in 2008. Other businesses have opened in the three strip-shopping centers. There are many local businesses in the area that offer a variety of goods and services.

New landscaping and a "Welcome to Temple" sign have recently been completed at the intersection of Highway 113 with Billings Road and Villa Rosa Road. This was done with a GATEway Grant which was awarded by the Georgia Department of Transportation in 2010. In 2011, the city received the annual Silver Award for Beautification for the gateway entrance into the city by the Environmental Projects Committee of the Carroll County Chamber of Commerce. Landscaping and sidewalks in front of existing businesses along Highway 113, near Interstate 20 have been added. A four-way pedestrian crosswalk has also been added.

The Downtown Development Authority is working to improve the downtown area. Arthur W. Petty is chairman of the Authority. Board members are Richard Bracknell, Lynn Ford, Doug Steadham, Jackie McWhorter, and Ginger Dufour.

The Temple Senior Center was completed in 2001 at 280 Rome Street. On June 7, 2004, it was named the Harry and Glenda Shadrix Complex. Sandra Stillwell is the director. A pavilion was built nearby. It was named the Powell-Luke Pavilion in honor of Luther Powell and Earl C. Luke, Sr. A play park for children was also built.

A new city gymnasium was opened in the fall of 2006 on Rome Street near the Senior Center. It is a 23,000-square foot double gymnasium with a large conference room. It was named in honor of Gene Yearty. The recreation department continues to grow. Thad Ferguson is the Recreation Director. There are eight ball fields, four tennis courts, and a practice football/soccer field. New SPLOST money from the county was used to acquire an additional 11.3 acres. A walking trail has also been completed. The city recently received a grant to help expand the recreation department.

The Major Temple Garden Club lot at the corner of James and Tallapoosa Streets has recently been made into a place of beauty. In 2007, the club was awarded a Community Foundation grant to help with underground wiring, a water system, etc. The club sponsors two annual plant sales and other projects during the year.

Several programs are available for those who have been hurt by the economy. Temple Area Christian United Ministries (TACUM) reaches out to families in need in our community. Also, the city, with the help of several organizations, sponsors a Backpack Program in which nonperishable food items and nourishing snacks are provided for needy children for the weekends.

Tim Shaw, Chief of Police, leads a police force of twelve officers. Equipment and training are upgraded as the budget allows. The Shop with a Cop Program is an annual Christmas event. Our water is purchased from Carroll County. The city operates a state-of-the-art sewer plant. In May 2012, the Temple Wastewater Treatment Plant won the "Platinum Award" from the Georgia Association of Water Professionals for being 100-percent compliant for five consecutive years.

Books which have been published in recent years by Temple authors or relating to the Temple area include: *'Tween WWII and Vietnam: A Georgia Farm Boy's Tour of Duty in the Air Force in the Early 1950's* by Donald Levans; *A Christmas Walk: Devotions for Advent* and *An Easter Walk from Palm Sunday to the Ascension* by Zan Marie Steadham; *Running on Full: The Story of Ruth and Ruby Crawford* by Neil Wilkinson; *Visions of God for Little Children* by Dr. Zane D. Chambers, Sr.; *Sweet and Sour Sushi on Life's Menu* by Lee Jones; *Sow, Weed, Water, Wait ...* by Delma Gine; *A Dog Named Munson Finds the Missing Game Ball* by Charlene Thomas; *Emily's*

Stitches: The Confessions of Thomas Calloway by Dr. Leverett Butts; *Death of Margaret Mitchell: The Tragedy Behind Gone With the Wind* by Gloria Gravitt Moulder; and *Blood of Cain, The Arcainians, Keezy's 10 Awesome Rules for Teenaged Dating* and *Milledgeville Misfit* by T.L. Gray.

Carolyn Gray created an exhibit detailing the education of African-American students in the county. She is president and CEO of the Carver High Museum and Archives of West Georgia. She and Ruth Holder were awarded plaques of appreciation for preserving local history by the Carroll County Historical Society at a ceremony on May 5, 2011.

A Temple Veterans' Memorial was built in front of the City Hall. The brick pathway honors veterans as well as public officials and those who work in public safety. The inscription reads, "Dedicated to the Veterans of Temple by the People of Temple" and dated October 16, 2004.

A sidewalk has been built on the south side of Sage Street from the fire station at Highway 78 to downtown. This project was funded by the Special Purpose Local Option Sales Tax monies.

The city recently approved an ordinance for the operation of golf carts within the city on a limited basis.

The 270-acre Little Tallapoosa Park held its Grand Opening in April 2012. It is located between Temple and Carrollton off Highway 113 near Sharp's Creek. It is a passive recreation site, dedicated to greenway preservation and featuring tent and RV camping, a paved and unpaved trail system that can be used by walkers, wildlife watchers, hikers, cyclists, and equestrians. Picnic pavilions are available, also.

Karen Powell operated the Potluck Museum at 311 Sage Street where the Farmers State Bank opened in 1912. The antiquated Mosler bank vault was the focus of the museum.

Rocky Branch Railroad and Ghost Town was located just off Hwy 78 on Center Point Road. It was owned and operated by Lisa Morrison. This attraction featured an Old West Town, a train ride, and a Pioneer Days Festival. Unfortunately, it closed in 2013.

Little Vine Petting Zoo, located at 757 Little Vine Road, specializes in Pony Parties, Pony Rides and Petting Zoo Parties for any event.

From an 1800s stagecoach route in the wilderness to a small Southern town, Temple has carved its place in Georgia history, and along the way proven what we've known all along: Temple is "West Georgia's best kept secret." We remain proud of our town and proud of our heritage.

An enormous debt of gratitude is due to those Temple citizens interviewed for the first version of this book in 1976. Their agile and sharp memories, pictures, and many documents proved a great boon to compiling this history. Many of these individuals had participated in the early building of the town, and it is through their labor and determination and unfailing optimism that Temple grew and flourished. With the passing of these remarkable people comes the concomitant loss of obtaining additional, first-hand historical accounts. This book is dedicated to those citizens. Also, many thanks to all who helped make this revision possible.

TEMPLE MAYORS

Courtesy, Max Stevens

Jesse Kinney (1822-1912), First Mayor of Temple

H.H. Sewell

W.B. Chandler

R.T. Williams

J.E. Edmondson

C.E. Ringer

C.L. Baskin

J.T. Brown

W.B. Manley

F.L. Young

J.T. West

Homer McColister

C.R. Hart

W.L. Adcock

Olin Johnson

L.T. Stevens

Herman Riggs

C.A. Truitt

W.L. Steadham, Jr.

L.L. Rainey

I.J. Holder

Homer Williams

Jeff Hansard   **Harry Shadrix**   **Lester Harmon**

Rick Ford

83½ Whitehall St.,
ATLANTA GA
Courtesy, Misses Pearl and Troy Lanier

Courtesy, Misses Pearl and Troy Lanier

Dr. Richard L. Rowe (1827-1902)   **Dr. James F. Brooks (1853-1893)**
These two gentlemen were Temple's first doctors.

Courtesy, Mrs. Ruby Kinney

Dr. C.L. Baskin   **Dr. John R. Turner**   **Dr. Behram Makulu**

Dr. Casper Lassetter, first graduate of Temple Model School, 1905, became an editor of *The Progressive Farmer* magazine.

Dr. Guy H. Wells, President of Georgia Southern College (1924-34), Georgia College (1934-1954)

Mrs. B.J. (Tallulah) McCain, Temple's first woman merchant, opened a millinery store in 1883.

Ira W. Williams, Organizer and Principal of Temple Model School, 1904.

**Laura Josephine Rozar,
Temple Model School Teacher,
organized the Northwest Georgia
High School Association in 1905.**

**Charles Thomas, Jr., Temple Attorney
and State Representative of 66th District**

**The Crawford twins wearing their familiar patriotic outfits at the
Peachtree Road Race in Atlanta**

Courtesy, Mrs. C.G. Smith

David Hamilton Carter, born in 1847, was the town marshal in 1900.

Courtesy, Mrs. Maggie Wynn Pope

Sage Street Stores, Circa 1908

Street Scene, Temple, Ga.

West Johnson Street Stores, Circa 1908

West Johnson Street, Circa 1908
Sign Reads: Tennessee Wagons, Kinney and Steadham

Sage Street Stores, Sycamore Trees and Town Well, Circa 1910

**Looking Over the Latest Automobiles,
Sage Street Stores Shaded by Sycamore Trees**

An Aerial View of Temple in 1936
1. Depot; 2. Post Office; 3. Methodist Church

Courtesy, Mrs. C.R. Hart

Sage Street, 1940s

Sage Street, 1953

Sage Street Stores, 1953

Moonshine still raided just north of Temple 1950s.
Remains of stills are common along area streams.

Abilene Baptist Church Baptism, Rev. Lawrence Akin, 1949

Remodeled Store Fronts, 1976

The Bank of Carroll County, located at 337 Sage Street, was built in 1976. It is currently the city hall.

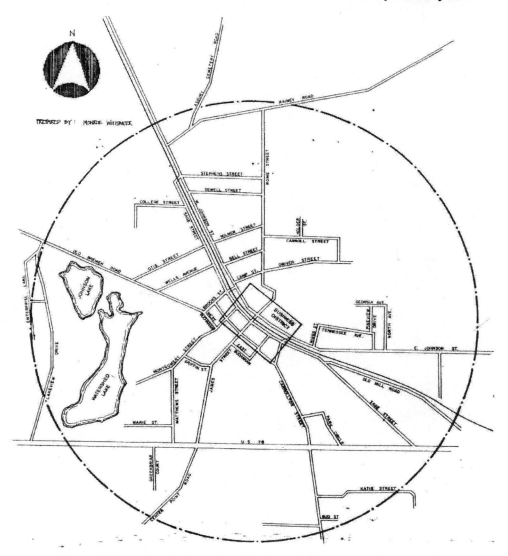

Map of Temple, Printed by Bank of Carroll County, 1976

Fire Station, Built in 1980

Temple Fire Truck, Bill Benton and Royce Henry, 1982

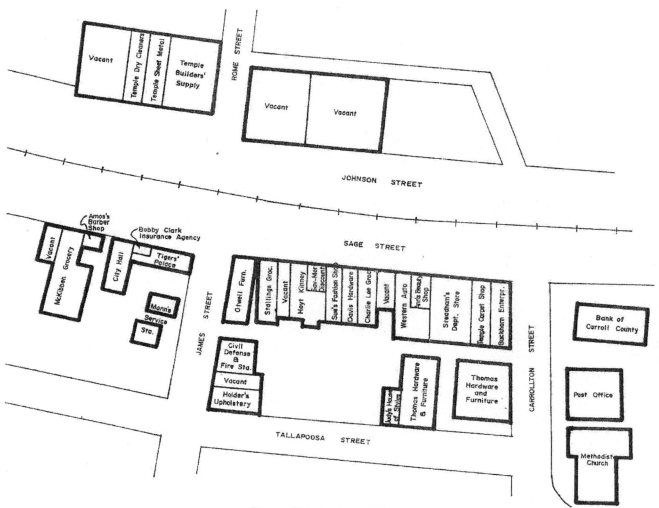

Store Occupants 1971

Masonic Lodge Hall, James Street

119

Sage Street, L.E.C. Stevens family outdoor kitchen and BBQ pit, used often in the 1940s and 1950s for family, church, and school socials.

**Ruins of Early Temple Jail Located on Rome Street
Behind the Johnson Street Stores**

Southern Depot, Temple, Ga.

Temple's Second Depot, Built in 1906
Architectural features include open trusses, a bay window, and eyebrow dormers.

Southern Railroad Depot

Bill McCain, Escar McCain, Carl Davis and Workmen, Circa 1899

**Southern Railway Train,
Ernest Lee (1894-1972)**

**Southern Railway Train, Jesse Kelly of
Hickory Level on Right**

Rev. William Brooks (1812-1887), and Catherine Brooks (1817-1897)
Rev. Brooks preached at Concord and Asbury Chapel Methodist Churches
before Temple was settled.

First Quarterly Conference, Center Point Methodist Church, 1904

Tent Meeting at Concord Methodist Church, 1919

Replica of Temple Methodist Church, First Brick Church Building in Carroll County, in Carroll County Centennial Parade, 1927

Asbury Chapel Built by the Major Temple Garden Club in 1947

This pyramidal structure stood at Asbury Cemetery until the 1940s. It was used for graveside services during inclement weather. The origin and rationale for the unique design is unknown to the author.

Temple Model School, 1904

One of the School Wagons.

Temple Model School Wagon, 1904
Olin Lovell (Driver), Phil Campbell, Sr. (Teacher)
Others include Lloyd Griffin, Rufus Davis, Walter Bartlett, Hiram Evans,
Clay and Clifton Allen, Loyal and Earl McColister

Courtesy, William Cown

Temple Model School Wagon, 1904
Included are Phil Astin, Sr., Paul Astin, Mattie Brooks, Harry Lou Smith,
Joe Smith, Minnie Newbern and Annie Brooks

Courtesy, William Cown

Model School Wagon, No. 3, Circa 1904

First Schoolmaster at Temple Academy, Lewis Connell, Mrs. Connell

Brooklyn School Pupils, Berry Yates, Teacher, Circa 1904

**County Line School, North of Center Point,
Paul Mote, Teacher, 1911**

Mt. Carmel School, 1914

Pine Grove School

Courtesy, Mrs. V.G. Johnston

Temple High School Students, 1914.
Uncle Giles Sumlin, Custodian; J.B. Parham, Principal

Courtesy, Mrs. Cecil Levans

Center Point School, 1914

Courtesy, Mrs. Ruby Kinney

Hickory Level School

Oak Grove School, Circa 1925-1926

Temple High School's Float in the Carroll County Centennial Parade in 1927

Courtesy, Mrs. Ovie Hamil

Temple High Graduating Class, 1928
Clyde Adams, Noble McBrayer, Mary Lou Hill, Roy Steadham, Kathleen Smith, Elvin
Kinney, Ovie McCain, Grady Parrish, Tom Stallings, Pearl Parrish, Eugene Kinney, Teacher
Virginia Lovvorn, Bertie Yearty, Principal Cranston Hamil

Courtesy, Virginia Tucker

John F. Brooks, Carroll County School Superintendent, 1929

Courtesy, Mrs. Erline Edmondson

First Class to Wear Caps and Gowns, 1936
L. to R., Frank Hart, Mattie Lou Garner, Mildred McBrayer, Erline Rabun, Betty Almon,
Julian Robinson, Sarah F. McGukin, Era Mae Kinney, Paul Riggs, Harry Bolden, Roderick
Rowe, Frank West, Winton Crutchfield, Bob Baskin, H.P. Bell, Principal

Courtesy, George Ferguson

First Senior Class to Take a Trip to Washington, D.C., 1937
L. to R., Merle Kinney, Lovie McBrayer, Lillian Truitt, George Ferguson, Eugene Teel,
Norman Wester, Lloyd Spence, Robert Dorough, Charles Thomas, Sr., John White

E.C. Karr's School Bus, 1938

Mrs. C.I. Holcombe's Second Grade, Temple School, 1938

Temple High School Seniors in Washington, 1939
Adrian Drew, Sara Riggs, Margaret Jacobs, Margaret Robinson, Gertrude Caldwell, Melba Adams, Faye Mathews, Faye Lambert, Melba Shadrix, Eugenia Gray, Andrew McGukin, Lowell Shockley, Roy Gray, Eldred Baskin, Mildred Baskin, Frank Lambert, Marian McBrayer, Martha Potate; W.O. Smith, Elmo Biggers, Teachers; E.C. Karr, Cecil Spence, Bus Drivers

Reproduction of Temple Model School Wagon in US Bicentennial Parade in Carrollton in 1976. Riders are Loyal Cobb, Paul Cobb, Nettie Riggs and Nan Pope.
Loyal Cobb was a rider of an original Model School wagon.

Bicentennial Painting by Temple Student Council at the Carroll County Court House

Temple High School Graduating Class, 1976
This was the last class to graduate from the 1939 school building.

Temple Primary School, 1982

Temple High School Senior Class of 1983
Leon Frost, Principal; Madeline Goza, Secretary;
Charlotte Doyal and Melissa Smith, Sponsors; Linda Boswell, Counselor

Brooklyn School Baseball Team, Circa 1906
Includes Jesse Cobb, Guy Green, Grady Barnes, Paul Roberts,
Paul Astin, Sam Astin and Harry Smith

Temple High School Basketball Team, 1927
Noble McBrayer, Raynor Potate, W. B. Manley,
Paul McBrayer, Grady Parrish, Charles White

Temple High School Basketball Team, 1951
Larry Potate, Jimmy Morrow, Billy Green, Bobby Ingram, Mac Hamil, Roy McClendon,
Kenneth Holt, Gene McGukin, George Spence, Coach Bill Thomas

1978 Temple Tigerettes, Girls Class B State Champions
Lorraine Spidell, Lynn Pope, Pam Billings, Donna Conaway, Esther Luke,
Diane Luke, Susan Holloman, Denise Dobbs, Tammie Drew, Coach Donald Stitcher,
Russell Shadrix and Joyce Levans, Managers

1946 Baseball Team
Front Row: Left to Right: Bill Thomas, Dumah Morris, Charles Thomas Sr., Ed Morris
Back Row: J.M. Holder, Herman Veich, Byron Lambert, J.D. Wester, Griffin Truitt,
Raynor Potate and Hoyt Steed

Unidentified Temple Ball Player
141

A Barn South of Temple, Late 1800s.
Included are Dave Williams, Warner Henry, Ed and Albert Pritchett and Grays

All Parties of whom we buy Cotton will be held Responsible for Water Packed, Damaged or Mixed Cotton.

W. A. ENTERKIN,

DEALER IN

Dry Goods, Groceries, Boots, Shoes, Hats, Crockery,

Hardware, Wagons and Buggies.

COTTON AND HIGH GRADE FERTILIZERS.

Temple, Ga., *Oct 18* 190 *0*

Bought of *O. M. McAlmon*

BALES COTTON.

Record of Payment of One Bale of Cotton
to Merchant W.A. Enterkin for a Debt Settlement

Clearing New Ground, Circa 1906
Mr. Hildebrand, Hubert Allen, George Allen, Unidentified, and Alcimus H. Allen

Demonstration Corn Crop, 1908
Includes J.W. Brooks, John F. Brooks, Brim Brooks, and S.M. Cown

Courtesy, William Cown

Georgia's First County Agent, S.M. Cown, 1908

Courtesy, Mrs. Joe Green

Wheat Field on Taylor's Gin Road, 1908
Mr. Crain, Myra Taylor Smith, Carl Taylor,
Alma Taylor Green, Neal Black and W.A. Taylor

144

**Monroe Burns in Local Cotton Field with
Sign Advertising Swift's Red Steer Fertilizer**

Oscar Durrett kept his cotton until the market improved.

Courtesy, Mrs. Earnest Smith

The cotton grew tall for Earnest Smith at Abilene, 1937.

Courtesy, Omer Muse

Grinding Sorghum Cane at Syrup Mill, Delone Muse, 1940

Yoked Oxen, Gene Black, 1940

Hickory Level Farm Scene, R.F. Turner, John R. Turner

Russell McGukin and Mark McGukin. Jack, the mule, is pulling corn planter, 1964.

**Dorough's Round Barn at Hickory Level,
Placed on the National Register of Historic Places in 1980.**

Hotel, Built in 1895

Courtesy, Roy Spruell

Dr. T.M. Spruell's Car, Ralph Spruell, Early 1900s

Temple Banking Company Ad, 1904

Courtesy, Roy Spruell

Brock Spruell, Raleigh Salesman

150

Early Road Machine. R.W. West, Overseer for Center Point Community, Zack Levans, Will Wester, Billie Almon, Newt West, Warren Crockett, Jack West, Emmett West, Homer Phillips, and Roy Almon

**Coca Cola Wagon (Villa Rica Electric Light and Power Co., Bottlers)
Boy seated became a prominent Temple druggist, Dr. C.R. Hart, early 1900s.**

151

England Beasley in John R. White's Drug Store, Circa 1914

Burn's Gin on West Johnson Street

Ed Perdue's Store, Joe Brown, Tom Morris, Arthur Kinney, Joe Green, Earl McColister, Homer Williams, Dr. L.E. Kinney (dentist), Lewis Brooks

Temple Hardware & Furniture Co.

Have recently added a complete line of Coffins, Caskets and other burial supplies. Can also serve the trade with new, beautiful auto Hearse, and will go anywhere on short notice. Will take great pleasure in rendering good service at moderate prices.

Don't forget us when in need of anything in the Furniture or Hardware line.

Temple Hardware & Furniture Co.
TEMPLE, GEORGIA

Temple Hardware and Furniture Co. Ad, 1921

Hickory Level Store. In 1927, the second floor housed Dr. S.F. Scales hospital.

Courtesy, Imogene Black Moore

Robert Franklin Pace
Gasoline Pump at Paces Store, Mt. Carmel, Circa 1930

Courtesy, Mrs. Selma Muse

E.D. "Doc" Mote
He sold Standard Oil products as well as fine food; hamburgers and cokes were 5 cents each,
Circa 1931.

Courtesy, Hoyt Steed

Steed Grocery
Hoyt Steed, J.M. "Barnyard" Holder, E.E. Steed, Annie Carnes, Lois Steed

Hart Drug Company, Circa 1940. The Temple Banking Company constructed this building in 1913. It is now Temple Pharmacy owned by Jim McWilliams.

Hart Drugstore
Dr. and Mrs. C.R. Hart, Eva McGinnis, 1940

Cartwright Store, The H.L. Cartwrights, Oscar Parrish

Jane West's 5&10 Cent Store on Sage Street, 1943-67

The Temple Theater, owned by the Hill family, was opened in 1946.

Courtesy, J.H. Thomas Family

Thomas Hardware and Furniture Store, Circa 1951

Bobby West's Store, 1954
Bruce Michael, J.M. "Barnyard" Holder, J.M. Rutledge

Masonic Lodge Hall, Rome Street

James Street Gulf Station

Burn's Western Auto Store on Sage Street

Caldwell's Store at Abilene, 1982

Courtesy, Mrs. Herman Riggs

Eldorado "Bud" Cobb Homeplace, Carrollton Street, Built in 1897

W.B. Manley Home, Sage Street at Old Bremen Road
Gib Williams, Gordon and Bethel Manley and Cleve Roop, 1899

Fletcher Otwell Family, County Line North of Center Point, Circa 1901

**Wells Family, (L. to R.), Cliff, J.C., Otis, Blanche and Claude.
"Surrey with Fringe on Top" in Background, Circa 1902**

Ralph Spruell and Pets, Early 1900s

In Charity Williams' day, no one smiled for the photographer.

Mattie, Willie and Bernie Kinney of Hickory Level in 1906. The fountain of water was unique for the area. Their father installed a system which pumped water from a creek.

Mrs. William Timmons. Blind Musicians Mattie, Ossie and Johnnie Timmons, 1908

Mr. and Mrs. W.C. Black, New Brooklyn Newlyweds, 1909

Courtesy, Mrs. Paul Cobb

McColister Home
Earl, Ulma, Loyal, Mary, W.F. and Homer, Circa 1910

Courtesy, Mrs. Dorothy A. Seals

Gordon Lee's Boys' Corn Club, 1911
Includes George Allen, Oliver Holcomb, Henry and Felton Shackleford

Courtesy, W.L. Adcock Family

Durrett Family Reunion at the Tom Durrett Home, Circa 1912

Courtesy, Mrs. Iva Hendrix

Abilene Group, Memorial Day, 1912, Carrollton.
Ella McKenzie Wilson, Nettie Jones Sims, Bessie Crutchfield, Vonie McKenzie,
Delphia Sharp Rowe, Iva Spence Hendrix, Mr. and Mrs. W.M. Spence

Courtesy, Roy Spruell

Annual Ford Picnic, Kingsberry Bridge at Carrollton

Courtesy, Mrs. Dova Cavender

Hickory Level Picnic Group, Kingsberry Bridge

Courtesy, Mrs. Lucy Bowen

L.E. Kinney and Friend at Webster Creek

Courtesy, Mrs. Virginia Tucker

Kinney Reunion at Smith's Hotel, Operated by the Ben Smiths, Circa 1922

Hiram Cooper and Georgie Turner

Dr. T.M. Spruell Home, 146 East Johnson Street
Ralph, Mrs. Spruell, Roy, Dr. Spruell, 1920s

Courtesy, Family of Earline W. Anderson

Mr. and Mrs. John R. White and their 1926 Whippet

Courtesy, Mrs. Cecil Levans

Elsie Levans, Cecil Levans and Ralph Wester

171

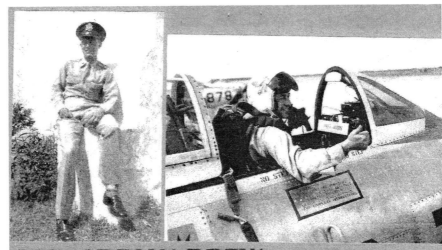

COL. ADRIAN DREW, valedictorian of Temple High School in 1939, **flew an Air force F101A and set a new world speed record in 1957.** He broke the previous record by Great Britain when L. P. Twiss piloted a Fairey Delta at 1,132.136 mph. He was awarded the Thompson Trophy for this, and the people of Temple honored him with a parade and Bar-B-Que.

Courtesy, Savonia Drew Hamil

Col. Adrian Drew flew an Air Force F101A and set a new world speed record in 1957.

Courtesy, Mrs. Iva Hendrix

Preparing for Annual Abilene Barbecue at Home of M.F. Hendrix, 1948, Raymond Williams and Manual Glanton

Major Temple Garden Club, 1950
From left to right: Lucille Burns, Kas Ferguson, Alice Adcock, Irma Hart, Hazel Lee,
Lenona Brown, Elizabeth Parrish, Bera McBrayer, Lula Potate, Betty Sewell
and TV Personality Julie Sanders

This photo of young Harold Walker Griffin was found
in the cornerstone of the Temple Model School.

173

BIBLIOGRAPHY

Books

Avery, I.W. *The History of the State of Georgia from 1850 to 1881.* New York: Brown and Derby Publishers, 1881.

Bell, John. *"Pickle It!": Minor League Baseball of Carrollton, Georgia.* Carrollton: Vabella Publishing, 2002.

Bonner, James C. *Georgia's Last Frontier.* Athens: University of Georgia Press, 1971.

Cheney, George F. *Carroll County Souvenir-Historical Edition.* Carrollton, Ga., privately printed, ca. 1910.

Cobb, Joe. *History of Carroll County.* Carrollton, Ga., ca. 1906.

Givens, William W. *The Centennial History of the Carrollton Baptist Association,* 1974.

Henderson, Ray. *The History of the Pony Club.* Lillum Press, 2011.

Holland, Robert H. *The Origin and Developments of Interscholastic Athletics Through the Georgia High School Association. Athens, Georgia, 1972.*

Krakow, Kenneth K. *Georgia Place-Names.* Macon: Winship Press, 1975.

Saye, Albert B. *Georgia History and Government* (textbook). Austin, Texas: Steck-Vaughn Company, 1973.

Tankersley, Allen P. *John P. Gordon: A Study in Gallantry.* Atlanta: The Whitehall Press, 1955.

Wiggins, Dr. David N. *Carroll and Haralson Counties in Vintage Postcards.* Charleston, SC: Arcadia Publishing, 2004.

Wilkinson, Neil. *Running on Full: The Story of Ruth and Ruby Crawford.* The Kennesaw State University Press, 2010.

_____, *Acts and Resolutions of the General Assembly of the State of Georgia,* 1882-1883. Atlanta: James P. Harrison and Company, Publishers, 1883.

_____, *Georgia State Gazetteer and Business Directory,* 1881-1882. Atlanta: James P. Harrison and Company, Publishers, 1881.

_____, *Memoirs of Georgia, Historical and Biographical.* 2 vols. Atlanta: Southern Historical Association, 1895.

_____, *Poor's Manual of Railroads, 1884.* New York: Charles M. Green Printing Company, 1884.

_____, *Carroll County Story as Told by the People, The.* Printed by Sesquicentennial Bicentennial Committee, Miss Edith Foster, Director of Neva Lomason Memorial Library, Chairman, 1976.

Manuscripts, Official and Unofficial

Registers of Charters, Carroll County, Book I, Office of the Clerk of Court, Carrollton
Carroll County Deed Books, Office of the Clerk of Court, Carrollton.

Carroll County Deed Books, Office of the Clerk of Court, Carrollton.

Register of Medical Practitioners, Carroll County, 1881-1976. Office of the Clerk of Court, Carrollton.

Educational History of Carroll County, 1871-1928. Scrapbook in the Office of the Carroll County Superintendent of Schools.

Ledgers of the Carroll County Board of Education. In the Office of the Carroll County Superintendent of Schools.

Minutes of the Carroll County Board of Education, 1929-1939. In the Office of the Carroll County Superintendent of Schools.

Pamphlets

Baker, John M. *A Sketch of a Trip to Europe made by J.M. Baker, Temple, Georgia.* Atlanta: Counts Printing Company, 1914.

Duggan, M.L. *Educational Survey of Carroll County.* Under Direction of Georgia Department of Education, 1918.

_____, *Model School, The.* Temple, Ga., ca. 1904.

_____, *Temple Graded School, Announcement.* Temple, Ga., ca. 1908.

_____, *Temple Public School,* Temple, Ga., ca. 1914.

Newspapers

Newspapers of West Georgia, The, 1877 - present. On microfilm at West Georgia College Library and West Georgia Regional Library. In the Office of the Ordinary of Carroll County. Author's Collection.

Atlanta Journal/Constitution, The, 1880 - present.

INDEX OF NAMES

Brooks family, 69
Brooks, J.F., 24
Brooks, J. F. (Dr.), 23
Brooks, J. W., 143
Brooks, James (Dr.), 22, 42
Brooks, James F. (Dr.), 14, 19, 108
Brooks, John, 69
Brooks, John F., 34,81, 87, 133, 143
Brooks, John Wesley, 92
Brooks, Lewis, 153
Brooks, Mattie, 69, 127
Brooks, Mattie (Cown), 81
Brooks, Nollie, 96
Brooks, William, 14, 55, 61,123
Brown, J. T., 87, 105
Brown, Joe, 153
Brown, Lenona, 173
Brown, Shanon, 48
Bryant, David, 14
Bryant, T. Oscar (Dr.), 42
Bryant, W. C. 63
Bryce, 61
Bryce, J. F., 61
Bryce, James, 61, 70
Burnham, Jimmy, 63
Burns, 152, 160
Burns, G. M., 54, 56, 93
Burns, Ken, 88
Burns, Lucille, 145, 173
Burns, Monroe, 63, 145
Burns, Mrs. G. M., 56
Burt, H. O., 56
Burton-Callaway, Dorothy, 41
Burton, Dorothy, 99
Burton, W. B., 63
Busbin, Artis, 63
Buttram, Earnest, 57
Butts, Leverett (Dr.), 102

Cain, E. J., 63
Caldwell, 27, 161
Caldwell, David, 56
Caldwell, Dewey, 56, 60
Caldwell, Gertrude, 136
Calhoun, W. M., 62
Camp, Otis, 34
Campbell and Bell, 23
Campbell, Danny, 69
Campbell, J. Phil, Sr., 34, 82
Campbell, J. Philander, 34
Campbell, Phil, Sr., 34, 69, 82, 126
Candler, Warren A. (Bishop), 61
Cannon, Weldon, 1
Cantrell, Jesse, 64
Carden, Danny, 88
Carmical, W. W. (Dr.), 42
Carnes, Annie, 155
Carnes, J. P., 14
Carroll, Charles, 4
Carroll, G. O., 63
Carroll, Gerald, 89
Carroll, J. L., 55
Carroll, Mrs. Julia, 39

Carroll, L. E., 88
Carroll, Lavonia, 55
Carswell, Miss Clara, 36
Carter, David Hamilton, 111
Carter, F. L., 63
Carter, President Jimmy, 89
Cartwright, Mrs. 86
Cartwright, H. L., 38, 78
Cartwright, Mrs. H. L., 157
Cartwright, Henry, 37
Cartwright, Wilson, 64
Cartwrights, 14
Cartwrights, H.L., 157
Cartwrights, The Henry, 86
Cash, 61
Cash, Bill, 88
Cash, Clair, 120, 173
Cash, Steve, 99
Cavender, Mrs. Dova, 122, 124, 168
Caylor, Max, 59
Chalkley, Mr. and Mrs. F. Eaton, 59
Chalkley, Susan Hayward, 59
Chambers, Zane D., Sr. (Dr.), 101
Chance, James, 15
Chance, Lottie Bell, 63
Chance, Mrs. Rena, 63
Chance, Verlie, 63
Chance, Warren, 64
Chandler, Allen D.(Gov.), 11
Chandler, W. B., 55, 87, 104
Chandler, William B., 55
Chandlers, 60
Chapman, Felton, 63
Chappell, E. M., 72
Chase, William J. J. 38
Cheek, Barbara, 78
Cheek, Nolan, 57, 78, 99
Church, Bobby (Rev.), 63
Clark, S., 63
Cline, Elwood, 63
Clonts, Glenn, 63
Coalson, A. J., 63
Cobb, A. C., 63
Cobb, Eldorado "Bud", 161
Cobb, Eldorado H., 48,
Cobb, I. O., 150
Cobb, Isaac E., 13, 14, 15, 81
Cobb, Miss Itty, 24
Cobb, Jesse, 139
Cobb, Joe, 70
Cobb, John T. (Dr.), 42
Cobb, Loyal, 34, 136
Cobb, Minnie T., 48
Cobb, Paul, 29, 32, 48, 69, 81, 136
Cobb, Mrs. Paul, 110, 126, 166
Cobb, W. M., 33
Cobb, Walker M., 47
Cole, 23, 71
Cole, Curtis, 64
Cole, F.J., 55
Cole, G. W., 55
Cole, Gilbert, 70
Cole, Gordon, 55

Cole, Mrs. Gordon, 31, 122
Cole, J. F., 55
Cole, Jeremiah, 70
Cole, Mary C., 55
Cole, R. L., 56
Cole, Robert, 56
Cole, S. V., 70
Coles, 60
Coltharp, 5
Collier, J. C., 63
Colquitt (Gov.), 21
Colquitt, A. H. (Gov.), 16
Conaway, 92
Conaway, Donna, 41, 140
Conaway, Gail, 99
Connell, Mrs., 128
Connell, E. L., 24, 33, 34, 87, 150
Connell, Mrs. E. L., 24
Connell, E. Lewis, 1, 24, 41
Connell. H. H., 63
Connell, John, 46
Connell, Lewis, 2, 29, 128
Connell, Miss Lil, 37
Conner, Max, 46, 57
Cook, Grover 62
Cook, Hamlin C., 46
Cook, Hamlin C. (Dr.) and John M.
   Allen, 24, 46
Cook, Hamlin C. (Dr.), 24
Cook, W. O., 63
Cooper, Hiram, 170
Copeland, 2, 23
Copeland, J. T., 23, 24
Copeland, John, 23
Costner, Angie, 100
Couch, James S., 56
Cown, 90, 92
Cown, Corinne, 92
Cown, Mattie (Brooks), 81
Cown, S. M, 81, 143,144
Cown, Sam, 69
Cown, William, 109, 127,143, 144
Crabb, James, 62
Craft, Eunice, 55
Craft, Harvey, 55
Crain, Mr., 144
Craven, Miss Myrtie, 47
Crawford, Dayton, 57
Crawford, Hamp, 64, 83
Crawford, Mr. and Mrs. Hamp, 81
Crawford, Henry F.
   (genealogy 9&10)
Crawford, Ruby, 78, 81, 89, 101, 110
Crawford, Ruth, 78, 81, 89, 101, 110
Crawford, W. J., 72
Creel, Benjamin, 59
Creel, Sarah, 60
Crews, A. B., 69
Crews, Alvin B., 48
Crisp, E.T., 17
Crocket, Sarah, 63
Crockets, 14
Crockett, Alice A., 59

Michael, John, 84
Miller, E. H, 62
Miller, Hiley, 100
Mims, Mike, 63
Mitchell, Bill, 33
Mitchell, Inez (Mrs.), 109
Mitchell, Margaret, 102
Mobley, 2, 23
Mobley, David H., 48
Mobley, Jethro A., 48
Montgomery, Alex (Col.), 22
Moore, Buna (Dr.), 46
Moore, Buna R. (Dr.), 42
Moore, G. F., 55, 84
Moore, George, 55
Moore, Imogene Black, 154
Moore, Lois, 55
Moore, M. J., 72
Moore, M. S., 63
Moore, Miss Ruth, 112
Morgan, J. D., 60
Morgan, Lucy D., 60
Morgan, Mary, 60
Morgan, S. E., 69
Morgan, Susan, 60
Morgan, T. R., 63
Morgan, William, 60
Morris, C. M., 93
Morris, Claude, 26, 85, 153
Morris, Claude M., 54
Morris, Dumah, 141
Morris, Ed, 141
Morris, Edward, 57
Morris, Frank, 69
Morris, Mary Beth, 55
Morris, Sandra, 41
Morris, Tom, 153
Morrison, Lisa, 102
Morrow, Earl, 40
Morrow, Jimmy, 140
Mote, E. D. "Doc", 155
Mote, Paul, 129
Mote, T. I., 56
Moulder, Gloria Gravitt, 102
Muse, 72
Muse, A. D., 56
Muse, Delone, 146
Muse, E. A., 60
Muse, Mrs. Elmira, 60
Muse, J. M., 60
Muse, Jessie, 70
Muse, Jessie W., 70
Muse, John, 60
Muse, Johnny, 48, 98, 99
Muse, M. E., 60
Muse, Mary, 60
Muse, Mrs. Merle Kinney, 113
Muse, Omer, 146
Muse, R. O., 55
Muse, Sef, 59, 70
Muse, Mrs. Selma, 155
Muse, W. P., 34, 35
Muse, Z. W., 60

Nalls, C. L., 62
Nash, Chancey, 41
Nesselhunt, Millard, 34
New, Eliza, 62
New, Nick, 62
Newbern, Minnie, 127
Newells, Lovett, 30
Newsome, Jack, 56, 70
Newsomes, The Jack, 73
Nolan, Miss Etta, 72
Nordholm, Henry, 55
Norman, W. B., 56
Norton, Mrs. Ruth, 109
Norton, Mrs.Vivian Chance, 63

O'Bryan Bros., 30
Ogletree, Susan Lipford, 41
Orr, (Dr.), 46
Ortenburg, Earnest A., 78
Ortenburg, Reba Smith, 78
Osborne, David, 48
Otwell, 50
Otwell, Miss Beatrice, 129
Otwell, Fletcher family, 162
Owens, Barry, 62

Pace, 64, 154
Pace, J. C., 63
Pace, James and Caroline, 60
Pace, Robert Franklin, 154
Palmer (Brother), 63
Palmer, L. D., 62
Palmer, Rick, 49, 50
Parham, J. B., 36, 41, 130
Parker, T. J., 62
Parks, Brad, 100
Parrish 51, 53, 73
Parrish, Mr. and Mrs., 73
Parrish, Mrs., 70
Parrish, (Captain), 70
Parrish, Claude, 57
Parrish, Elizabeth, 173
Parrish, Gary, 29, 99
Parrish, Grady, 133, 139
Parrish, Jimmy, 73
Parrish, Lawrence, 73
Parrish, Oscar, 157
Parrish, Pearl, 133
Parrish, Ralph, 73
Parrish, Roy, 53, 73
Parrish, Sara, 29
Parrishes, 73
Perdue, Ed, 153
Perkins, Ermus, 62
Perkins, G. W., 62
Petty, Arthur, 101
Phillips, Mr., 23
Phillips, Carlin, 64
Phillips, Homer, 71, 151
Phillips, Susan, 63
Phillips, Wesley, 62
Pierce and Baskin, 70

Pierce, (Bishop), 61
Poe, Edgar Allen, 88
Pointer, Pam, 39
Pollard, Mrs., 70
Pollard, Stephen, 87
Pope, Bobby, 41, 88
Pope, Jane, 99
Pope, Kim, 100
Pope, Lynn, 41, 140
Pope, Mrs. Maggie Wynn, 111
Pope, Nan, 136
Pope, Ray, 88
Potate, Larry, 140
Potate, Lula, 173
Potate, Martha, 136
Potate, Raynor, 139, 141
Powell, 61
Powell, Darnell, 99
Powell, Donn, 62
Powell, Karen, 46, 102
Powell, Levi Thomas Gardner, 61
Powell, Luther, 101
Powell, Thomas G. (Rev.), 70
Powell, William Francis Spaight, 61
Prichard, W. C., 78
Prince, Gillis, 62
Pritchett, Ed and Albert, 142

Rabun, Erline, 134
Raburn, Mr. and Mrs. Hoyt, 72
Raburn, Mrs. Hoyt, 72
Raburn, James and Caroline, 60
Raburn, Mrs. Pearl, 92
Raburn, Tommy, 36
Raburn, W. L., 55
Raburn, W.T. 57
Ragsdale, Louise, 63
Ragsdale, Sharon, 63
Ragsdale, Y. B., 63
Ragsdale, Mr. and Mrs. Y. B., 63
Rainey, L. L., 87, 106
Rainey, Mrs. Lula, 63
Ray, Rachael, 89
Redding, Jimmy, 56
Redding, Katherine, 39
Redding, Robert, 56
Reeves, H.E., 30
Reeves, Joel, 59
Reeves, Mrs. Ruby, 56
Reid, Mr.and Mrs. Hoyatt, 60
Reid, Miss Tassie, 41
Reids, 60
Reynolds, H. B., 63
Richards and Associates, 40
Richards, Roy and Hugh, 78
Riggs, (Rev. Mr.), 14
Riggs, A.H., 23
Riggs and Brooks, 23
Riggs, A. V., 63
Riggs, Herman, 87, 106
Riggs, Mrs. Herman, 161
Riggs, J. D and A.H., 23
Riggs, J. Q., 24

Riggs, J. V., 63
Riggs, John, Jane and Sara, 60
Riggs, Nettie, 84, 136
Riggs, Paul, 134
Riggs, Sara, 136
Ringer, Benjamin F., 14, 18
Ringer, C. E., 55, 105
Ringer, Clarence E., 87
Ringer, G. C., 55
Roberson, Bonnell, 39
Roberson, Jim, 62
Roberts, Miss Crawford, 41
Roberts, Paul, 139
Roberts, S.W. Sr., 85
Roberts, Mrs. S. W., Sr., 139, 162
Robinson, Earl, 57
Robinson, Jesse, 64
Robinson, Julian, 134
Robinson, Margaret, 136
Robinson, N. T., 55
Robinson, Odie Bell, 46
Rogers, Denzil, 41
Rogers, Sammy, 55
Rogers, Terry, 60
Roop, Cleve, 162
Roop, G. W., 33
Roop, W. W., 63
Roosevelt, Franklin (Pres.), 38
Ross, N. J., 63
Roush, C. A. and Associates, 54
Rowe, 2, 23, 46
Rowe, (Dr.), 14
Rowe, Miss Bessie, 46
Rowe, Delphia Sharp, 167
Rowe, J. P., 57
Rowe, John, 83
Rowe, R. L., 55
Rowe, Richard, 22
Rowe, Richard L., 14, 47
Rowe, Richard L. (Dr.), 19, 42, 108
Rowe, Roderick, 134
Rowe, Rufus, 62
Rowe, W. L., 55
Rozar, Mrs. L. J., 41
Rozar, Laura J., 35
Rozar, Laura Josephine, 34, 82, 110
Rush, Molly, 23
Rutledge, "Bud", 68
Rutledge, Danny, 99
Rutledge, Fred, 68
Rutledge, J.M., 83, 159
Rutledge, Martell, 63
Rutledge, Pam, 159
Rutledge, S. M., 63
Rutledge, Thomas "Bud", 68
Rutledge, W. Oscar, 68

Sanders, Carl (Gov.), 57
Sanders, Julie, 173
Saul, Joseph L., 26, 89
Scales, John, 62
Scales, Kansas, 46
Scales, Ray, 62

Scales, S. Frank (Dr.), 70
Scales, S. F. (Dr.), 86, 154
Scott, Eudell, 36
Scott, George, 62
Seals, Mrs. Dorothy A., 143, 166
Senft, Barbara, 99
Sewell, 2, 24, 53,78, 88, 98, 99
Sewell, Betty, 173
Sewell, H. H., 87, 104
Sewell, Mrs. H. H., 56
Sewell, Hamp, 33, 98
Sewell, Hampton H., 81
Sewell, Miss Maude E., 48
Sewell, P. I., 23, 24, 64
Sewell, Roy S., 53
Shackleford, Henry and Felton, 166
Shackleford, T. H., 41
Shackleford, W. R., 63
Shackleford, Mr. and Mrs. W. Z., 63
Shadix, J. W., 41
Shadrix, C. W., 56
Shadrix, Glenda, 101
Shadrix, H. M., 56
Shadrix, Harry, 41, 87, 88, 89,
   99,101,107
Shadrix, Kenneth, 56
Shadrix, Melba, 136
Shadrix, Russell, 140
Shadrix, Terry, 57
Shanks, Charles, 40
Sharp, 15
Sharp, G.A., 29
Sharp, Gordon, 56
Sharp, H. T.,72
Sharp, Hiram,70
Sharp, Uncle Hiram, 70
Sharp, J. O., 72
Sharps, 70, 72, 102
Shaw, Tim, 101
Sheets, Grover, 63-64
Sheets, Herschel (Rev), 59
Shelton, W. A., 35, 41
Shepard, Hugh, 55
Shepard, W. H., 55
Sherman, 19
Shirah, C. B., 63
Shirah, Mr. and Mrs. James B., 68
Shirah, N. R., 63
Shockley, Lowell, 136
Shockley, Miss Lucile, 69
Sikes, Ronald D., 41
Simmons, William, 100
Simms, William Gilmore, 88
Simpkins, R. D., Sr., 55
Sims, Mr. and Mrs. Howard, 128
Sims, Howard, B., 48
Sims, John, 24, 31
Sims, Nettie Jones, 167
Sims, Robert T., 48
Sims, Samuel, 62
Smith, Mr. and Mrs. Alfred I., 61
Smith, Mrs. C.G., 111
Smith, Dennis, 62

Smith, Earnest, 146
Smith, Mrs. Earnest , 146
Smith, Harry, 139
Smith, Harry Lou, 127
Smith, Miss Hazel, 37
Smith, Hoke (Honorable), 32
Smith, J. G., 54
Smith, Joe, 127
Smith, John, 70
Smith, Kathleen, 133
Smith, L. K., 78
Smith, Lois, 36
Smith, Melissa, 41, 138
Smith, Myra Taylor, 144
Smith, Oscar, 69
Smith, Miss Ruth, 69
Smith, W. O., 38, 41, 136
Smith, Winfred, 52
Smith, Wyot M., (Dr.), 42
Smiths, The Ben, 169
Snead, A.K., 54, 150
Spear, Claudia, 37
Spear, L. D., 37
Spearman, F. G., 41
Spence, Mr., 72
Spence and McCalman, 72
Spence and Muse, 72
Spence, C. H., 56
Spence, Cecil, 36, 38, 83, 136
Spence, G. F., 60
Spence, George, 140
Spence, George F., 70
Spence, Hiram, 70
Spence, J. R., 24, 72
Spence, L.C., 72
Spence, Leon, 70
Spence, Mrs. Leon, 70
Spence, Lloyd, 134
Spence, M.E.V., 72, 92
Spence, W. H., 55
Spence, Mr. and Mrs. W. M., 167
Spence, W. M., "Billy", 70
Spence, William M.
   (genealogy 10&11)
Spencer, J. W., 63
Spences, 72
Spidell, Lorraine, 41, 140
Spinks, J. M., 63
Spruell, (Dr.), 45, 46, 170
Spruell, Mrs., 170
Spruell, Brock, 150
Spruell, Ralph, 149, 163, 170
Spruell, Roy, 45, 149, 150, 163, 168,
   170
Spruell, T. M., 34, 86
Spruell, T. M. (Dr.), 45, 86, 149, 170
Spruell, Thompson M., (Dr.), 42
Stallings, C. E., 38, 55
Stallings, C. T., 55
Stallings, Charley E., 48
Stallings, Harrison, 57
Stallings, J. M. D., 63
Stallings, Mary E., 63

ABOUT THE AUTHORS

Burell Williams Holder, the son of Isaac J. Holder and Edith Marie (Carnes) Holder, was born in DeKalb County, Georgia, on February 21, 1927. His father was a road master for the Seaboard Railroad. His brothers and sister are Floyd, Hazel, Hoyt, Marion, and Lamar.

In 1930, the family moved to Cuthbert, Georgia and then to Montgomery, Alabama in 1933. Upon Isaac Holder's retirement in 1939, the family moved to Temple, Georgia.

The author was educated in the Montgomery and Temple Public Schools, West Georgia College and the University of Georgia. During World War II he served in the U.S. Navy. He began his teaching career in 1950 at Winder High School, Winder, Georgia. Beginning in1951, he served as a classroom teacher and administrator in the Carroll County School system. In 1952, he was married to Eva Ruth Roberts of the Flat Rock community, Carroll County.

Ruth Roberts Holder, the daughter of Samuel Watson Roberts, Sr., a farmer, and Claire Otwell Roberts, was born in the Flat Rock community near Villa Rica. Her brothers are Robert Glenn Roberts and the late Samuel Watson Roberts, Jr. She was educated in the Flat Rock and Villa Rica Schools, West Georgia College, and the University of Georgia where she earned a B.S.Ed., an M.Ed., and her Ed.S., respectively. In 1952, she married B. W. Holder. She served as a teacher and librarian in the Paulding and Carroll County School Systems and retired in 1993 after forty years of service. She and her husband, the late B. W. Holder, authored their first history on Temple in 1976 (updated in 1982).